Collins Dutch phrasebook

Consultant
Madeleine Lee

First published 1993
This edition published 2007

Reprint 10 9 8 7 6 5 4 3 2 1 0
Typeset by Davidson Pre-Press, Glasgow
Printed in Malaysia by Imago

www.collins.co.uk

ISBN 13 978-0-00-724667-0
ISBN 10 0-00-724667-6

Using your phrasebook

Your *Collins Gem Phrasebook* is designed to help you locate the exact phrase you need, when you need it, whether on holiday or for business. If you want to adapt the phrases, you can easily see where to substitute your own words using the dictionary section, and the clear, full-colour layout gives you direct access to the different topics.

The Gem Phrasebook includes:

- Over 70 topics arranged thematically. Each phrase is accompanied by a simple pronunciation guide which eliminates any problems pronouncing foreign words.

- A Top ten tips section to safeguard against any cultural faux pas, giving essential dos and don'ts for situations involving local customs or etiquette.

- Practical hints to make your stay trouble free, showing you where to go and what to do when dealing with everyday matters such as travel or hotels and offering valuable tourist information.

- Face to face sections so that you understand what is being said to you. These example mini-dialogues give you a good idea of what to expect from a real conversation.

- Common announcements and messages you may hear, ensuring that you never miss the important information you need to know when out and about.

- A clearly laid-out 3000-word dictionary means you will never be stuck for words.

- A basic grammar section which will enable you to build on your phrases.

- A list of public holidays to avoid being caught out by unexpected opening and closing hours, and to make sure you don't miss the celebrations!

It's worth spending time before you embark on your travels just looking through the topics to see what is covered and becoming familiar with what might be said to you.

Whatever the situation, your *Gem Phrasebook* is sure to help!

Contents

Pronouncing Dutch

The syllable to be stressed is marked in **bold**.

b, **d**, **f**, **h**, **l**, **m**, **n**, **ng** (combination), **s**, **z** like English
d at the end of a word usually sounds like 't'
n in words ending -**en** is often not pronounced properly, with the **e** before it sounding like 'u' (as in Arthur)
k, **p**, **t** like English but not aspirated
r like English but more rolled
v like English but more aspirated
w like English 'v' but less aspirated

Dutch vowels can have short and long sounds.

Dutch	sounds like	example	pronunciation
a	smart	mast	mast
a/aa	ah	straten/maat	**strah**-tu/maht
e	best	best	best
e	Arthur	de	du
e/ee	may	negen/zee	**nay**-CHu/zay
ei/ij	**ei** – no equivalent in English, try the **i** in r**i**ce, but a bit longer		
eu	**eu** – no equivalent in English, try the **ea** in **ea**rly but a bit longer, with rounded lips pointing forward		

Pronouncing Dutch

Dutch	sounds like	example	pronunciation
i	it	**witte**	**wit**-tu
ie	feet	**niet**	neet
o	top, short	**kort**	kort
o/oo	oh	**groot/boot**	CHroht/boht
oe	foot	**moet**	moot
ou/au	how	**jou/nauw**	yow/now
u	**ue** – no equivalent in English, try the **u** in c**u**e or French m**u**sée, but shorter		
u/uu	**uu** – no equivalent in English, try the **u** in h**u**ge or French m**u**sée, but longer		
ui	**ui** – no equivalent in English, try the **ow** in n**ow** followed by a short **i** sound		
g/ch	loch	**mag/tochten**	maCH/**toCH**-tu
j	yes	**ja**	yah
sj	short	**meisje**	**mei**-shu
sch	**sCH** – no equivalent in English: **s** and **CH** in rapid succession		

Top ten tips

1 The service charge for dining at restaurants is included in the price of the meal. If you are happy with the service, a small tip (around 10%) is appreciated.

2 Holland is actually a region in the central-western part of The Netherlands. Don't call The Netherlands Holland.

3 Waving your hand, palm open, parallel to your ear means something is delicious (**lekker**)

4 It is considered rude to leave the table during dinner (even to go to the bathroom).

5 Everybody from the age of 14 is required to be able to show a valid identity document to police officers at their request.

6 The Dutch are very reserved about their private lives, so don't ask personal questions.

7 When you are a guest at a birthday, wedding, or graduation party, congratulate each family member on their relation's birthday, wedding, or graduation.

8 The Dutch answer the telephone saying their last name preceded by the word '**met**' (with).

9 When arriving at someone else's house, it is considered impolite to step in the house without being asked to do so.

10 Invitations and promises are taken literally, so don't promise anything you can't deliver.

Talking to people

Hello/goodbye, yes/no

You will often find the Dutch quite formal in their greetings, shaking hands both on meeting and parting. You should use the formal **u** for 'you' unless you know the person you are talking to quite well (or you are talking to a child).

Yes	**Ja** yah
No	**Nee** nay
OK!	**O.K.** oh-**kay**
Please	**Alstublieft** als-tuu-**bleeft**
Don't mention it	**Graag gedaan** CHrahCH CHu-**dahn**
With pleasure!	**Graag** CHrahCH
Thank you	**Dank u** dank uu

Thanks very much	**Dank u wel** dank uu wel
No, thank you	**Nee, dank u** nay, dank uu
Sir/Mr	**Meneer** mu-**nayr**
Madam/Mrs/Ms	**Mevrouw** mu-**vrow**
Miss	**Mejuffrouw** mu-**yuef**-frow
Hello!	**Hallo!** hal-**loh!**
Goodbye!	**Dag!** daCH!
Good morning	**Goedemorgen** **CHoo**-du-mor-CHu
Good afternoon	**Goedemiddag** **CHoo**-du-mid-daCH
Good evening	**Goedenavond** **CHoo**-du-ah-vont
Good night	**Goedenacht** **CHoo**-du-naCHt
See you tomorrow	**Tot morgen** tot **mor**-CHu
See you later	**Tot straks** tot straks
Excuse me!/Pardon	**Pardon!** par-**don**!

Excuse me (sorry)	**Het spijt me** ut speit mu
How are you?	**Hoe gaat het met u?** hoo CHaht ut met uu?
Fine, thanks	**Goed, dank u** CHoot, dank uu
And you?	**En met u?** en met uu?
I don't understand	**Ik begrijp het niet** ik bu-**CHreip** ut neet
Do you speak English?	**Spreekt u Engels?** spraykt uu **eng**-els?

Key phrases

The easiest way to ask for something is by naming what you want and adding the word for please, **alstublieft**.

the (common gender)	**de** du
the (neuter)	**het** ut
a/one	**een/één** un (unstressed)/ayn (stressed)
the cup	**de kop** du kop

the station	**het station** ut sta-**shon**
two cups of coffee	**twee koppen koffie** tway **kop**-pu **kof**-fee
a lager, please	**een pils, alstublieft** un pils, als-tuu-**bleeft**
a bottle of wine, please	**een fles wijn, alstublieft** un fles wein, als-tuu-**bleeft**
my...	**mijn...** mein...
my name	**mijn naam** mein nahm
my passport	**mijn paspoort** mein **pas**-pohrt
your...	**uw...** uuw...
your name	**uw naam** uuw nahm
your passport	**uw paspoort** uuw **pas**-pohrt
Do you have...?	**Heeft u...?** hayft uu...?
Do you have milk?	**Heeft u melk?** hayft uu melk?
Do you have a room?	**Heeft u een kamer?** hayft uu un **kah**-mer?
Do you have a town map?	**Heeft u een plattegrond?** hayft uu un plat-tu-**CHront**?

I'd like...	**Ik wil graag...** ik wil CHrahCH...
I'd like an ice cream	**Ik wil graag een ijsje** ik wil CHrahCH un **eis**-shu
I'd like a table	**Ik wil graag een tafel** ik wil CHrahCH un **tah**-fel
I'd like cheese	**Ik wil graag kaas** ik wil CHrahCH kahs
We'd like...	**Wij willen graag...** wei **wil**-lu CHrahCH...
We'd like two pizzas	**Wij willen graag twee pizzas** wei **wil**-lu CHrahCH tway pizzas
More...	**Meer...** mayr...
More bread	**Meer brood** mayr broht
More water	**Meer water** mayr **wah**-ter
Another...	**Nog een...** noCH un...
Another bottle	**Nog een fles** noCH un fles
Another glass	**Nog een glaas** noCH un CHlas
How much is it?	**Hoeveel is het?** **hoo**-vayl is ut?
How much does it cost?	**Wat kost dat?** wat kost dat?

large	**groot** CHroht
small	**klein** klein
with	**met** met
without	**zonder** **zon**-der
Where is...?	**Waar is...?** wahr is...?
Where are...?	**Waar zijn...?** wahr zein...?
Where is the station?	**Waar is het station?** wahr is ut sta-**shon**?
Where are the toilets?	**Waar zijn de toiletten?** wahr zein du twa-**let**-tu?
How do I get...?	**Hoe kom ik...?** hoo kom ik...?
to the station	**bij het station** bei ut sta-**shon**
to the centre (of town)	**in het centrum** in ut **sen**-truem
There is/are...	**Er is...** er is...
There isn't/ aren't any...	**Er is geen...** er is CHayn...
When...?	**Wanneer...?** wan-**nayr**...?

What time is...?	**Hoe laat is...?** hoo laht is...?
today	**vandaag** van-**dahCH**
tomorrow	**morgen** **mor**-CHu
Can I...?	**Kan ik...?** kan ik...?
Can I smoke?	**Kan ik roken?** kan ik **roh**-ken?
Can I pay?	**Kan ik betalen?** kan ik bu-**tah**-lu?
How does this work?	**Hoe werkt dit?** hoo werkt dit?
What does this mean?	**Wat betekent dit?** wat bu-**tay**-kent dit?

Signs and notices

heren	gents
dames	ladies
zelfbediening	self-service
open	open
gesloten	closed
duwen	push
trekken	pull

niet op het ijs	do not step on the ice
kassa	cash desk
bagage	luggage
betaal aan de kassa	pay at the cash desk
informatie	information
spoor/perron	platform (train)
toiletten	toilets
vrij	free, vacant
bezet	engaged
buiten dienst	out of order/not in service
te huur	for hire/to rent
te koop	for sale
verkoop	sales
uitverkoop	sale
kelder	basement
begane grond	ground floor
ingang	entrance
uitgang	exit
geen ingang	no entry
nooduitgang	emergency exit
kaarvertkoop	ticket office
privé	private
datum	date
lift	lift
heet	hot
warm	warm
koud	cold
kamers vrij	vacancies

vol	no vacancies
EHBO	casualty department/ first aid post
ongevallen	casualty department
niet aanraken	do not touch
zwemmen gevaarlijk	swimming dangerous
zwemmen verboden	no swimming
roken	smoking
niet roken alstublieft	no smoking please

Polite expressions

The meal was delicious	**Het was lekker** ut was **lek**-ker
Enjoy your meal	**Eet smakelijk** ayt **smah**-ku-luk
This is a gift for you	**Dit is een cadeau voor jou (u)** dit is un **kah**-doh vohr yow (uu)
Pleased to meet you	**Aangenaam kennis te maken** **ahn**-CHu-nahm **ken**-nis tu **mah**-ku
Thanks for your hospitality	**Bedankt voor uw gastvrijheid** bu-**dankt** vohr uuw **CHast**-vrei-heit
Thank you very much	**Dank u wel** dank uu wel

Celebrations

Merry Christmas! **Vrolijk Kerstfeest!**
vroh-luk **kerst**-fayst!

Happy New Year! **Gelukkig Nieuwjaar!**
CHu-**luek**-kiCH **nee**-yoo-yahr!

A good trip! **Goede reis!**
CHoo-du reis!

Cheers! **Proost!**
prohst!

Congratulations! (having a baby, getting married, etc.) **Gefeliciteerd!**
CHu-**fay**-lee-see-tayrt!

Making friends

In this section we have used the familiar form **je** for the questions.

FACE TO FACE

A **Hoe heet jij?**
hoo hayt yei?
What's your name?

B **Ik heet...**
ik hayt...
My name is...

A **Waar kom je vandaan?**
wahr kom yu van-**dahn**?
Where are you from?

B **Ik ben Engels. Ik woon in Londen**
ik ben **eng**-els. ik wohn in **lon**-du
I am English. I live in London

A **Aangenaam kennis te maken!**
ahn-CHu-nahm **ken**-nis tu **mah**-ku!
Pleased to meet you!

How old are you?	**Hoe oud ben je?** hoo owt ben yu?
I'm ... years old	**Ik ben ... jaar** ik ben ... yahr
Are you Dutch? (male/female)	**Ben je Nederlander (Nederlandse)?** ben yu **nay**-der-lan-der (**nay**-der-land-su)?
I'm English/ Scottish/Welsh (male/female)	**Ik ben Engelsman (Engelse)/ Schot (Schotse)/Welsh** ik ben **eng**-els-man (**eng**-el-su)/ sCHot (**sCHot**-su)/welsh
I live in London	**Ik woon in Londen** ik wohn in **lon**-du
We live in Glasgow	**Wij wonen in Glasgow** wei **woh**-nu in **glas**-goh
I'm still studying	**Ik studeer nog** ik stuu-**dayr** noCH
I work	**Ik werk** ik werk

I'm retired	**Ik ben gepensioneerd** ik ben CHu-pen-see-oh-**nayrt**
I'm...	**Ik ben...** ik ben...
single	**vrijgezel** **vrei**-CHu-zel
married	**getrouwd** CHu-**trowt**
divorced	**gescheiden** CHu-**sCHei**-du
I have...	**Ik heb...** ik heb...
a boyfriend	**een vriend** un vreent
a girlfriend	**een vriendin** un vreen-**din**
a partner	**een partner** un **part**-ner
I have ... children	**Ik heb ... kinderen** ik heb ... **kin**-du-ru
I have no children	**Ik heb geen kinderen** ik heb CHayn **kin**-du-ru
I'm here...	**Ik ben hier...** ik ben heer...
on holiday	**op vakantie** op vah-**kan**-see
for work	**om te werken** om tu **wer**-ku

> **Leisure/interests** (p 67) > **Sport** (p 74)

Work

What work do you do?	**Wat voor werk doet u?** wat vohr werk doot uu?
Do you enjoy it?	**Vindt u het leuk?** vint uu ut leuk?
I'm...	**Ik ben...** ik ben...
a doctor	**dokter/arts** **dok**-tur/arts
a teacher (male/female)	**leraar/lerares** **le**-rahr/le-rah-**res**
I work from home	**Ik werk thuis** ik werk tuis
I'm self-employed	**Ik ben zelfstandig ondernemer** ik ben zelf-**stan**-diCH on-der-**nay**-mer

Weather

zonnig **zon**-niCH	sunny
regen **ray**-CHu	rain
mist mist	mist/fog
bewolkt bu-**wolkt**	cloudy

It's sunny	**De zon schijnt** du zon sCHeint
It's raining	**Het regent** ut **ray**-CHent
It's snowing	**Het sneeuwt** ut **snay**-oot
It's windy	**Het waait** ut **wah**-eet
What a lovely day!	**Wat een mooie dag!** wat un **moh**-ee-yu daCH!
It's very hot	**Het is erg heet** ut is erCH hayt
What will the weather be like tomorrow?	**Wat voor weer krijgen we morgen?** wat vohr wayr **krei**-CHu wu **mor**-CHu?
Will it rain?	**Gaat het regenen?** CHaht ut **ray**-CHu-nu?
Will it snow?	**Gaat het sneeuwen?** CHaht ut **snay**-wu?
Will there be a storm?	**Komt er storm?** komt er storm?
What is the temperature?	**Wat is de temperatuur?** wat is du tem-pu-rah-**tuur**?
Is the ice strong enough for skating?	**Is het ijs sterk genoeg om te schaatsen?** is ut eis sterk CHu-**nooCH** om tu **sCHaht**-su?

Getting around

Asking the way

tegenover tay-CHun-**oh**-ver	opposite
naast nahst	next to
vlakbij **vlak**-bei	near to
stoplichten, de **stop**-liCH-tu	traffic lights
op de hoek op du hook	at the corner
rechtdoor **reCHt**-dohr	straight on
links links	left
rechts reCHts	right
terug te-**rueCH**	back

FACE TO FACE

A **Pardon meneer/mevrouw! Hoe kom ik bij het station?**
par-**don** mu-**nayr**/mu-**vrow**! hoo kom ik bei ut sta-**shon**?
Excuse me sir/madam! How do I get to the station?

B **Ga rechtdoor, na de kerk gaat u linksaf/rechtsaf**
CHah **reCHt**-dohr, nah du kerk CHaht uu **link**-saf/ **reCHt**-saf
Go straight on, after the church turn left/right

A **Is het ver?**
is ut ver?
Is it far?

B **Nee, vijfhonderd meter/drie minuten lopen**
nay, **veif**-hon-dert **may**-ter/dree mee-**nuu**-tu **loh**-pu
No, 500 metres/three minutes' walk

A **Dankjewel!**
dank-yu-**wel**!
Thank you!

B **Graag gedaan!**
CHrahCH CHu-**dahn**!
You're welcome!

We're looking for...	**Wij zoeken...** wei **zoo**-ku...
Can I walk there?	**Kan ik er heen lopen?** kan ik er hayn **loh**-pu?
We're lost	**Wij zijn verdwaald** wei zein ver-**dwahlt**
Is this the right way to...?	**Is dit de goede weg naar...?** is dit du **CHoo**-du weCH nahr...?
How do I get onto the motorway?	**Hoe kom ik op de autoweg?** hoo kom ik op du **ow**-toh-weCH?

Can you show me where it is on the map?	**Kunt u mij laten zien waar het is op de kaart?** kuent uu mei **lah**-tu zeen wahr ut is op du kahrt?

YOU MAY HEAR...	
Na de brug nah du brueCH	After the bridge
Ga linksaf/rechtsaf CHah **link**-saf/**reCHt**-saf	Turn left/right

Bus and coach

For local Dutch public transport you will often need to buy a multiple-journey card (10 or more journeys) called a **strippenkaart**. You can buy these from ticket machines and at post office counters and stamp them for the required number of zones in a ticket-reading machine when you get on. On buses and trams, small **strippenkaarten** for single journeys can be bought from the driver, but it is cheaper to buy them in advance.

FACE TO FACE

A **Pardon, welke bus gaat naar het vliegveld?**
par-**don**, wel-ku bues CHaht nahr ut **vleeCH**-velt?
Excuse me, which bus goes to the airport?

B **Nummer zestien**
nuem-mer **zes**-teen
Number 16

A **Waar is de bushalte?**
wahr is du **bues**-hal-tu?
Where is the bus stop?

B **Daar, rechts**
dahr, reCHts
There, on the right

A **Waar kan ik een (strippen)kaart kopen?**
wahr kan ik un **strip**-pu-kahrt **koh**-pu?
Where can I buy a (multiple-use) ticket?

B **Bij de kaartautomaat of aan het loket**
bei du **kahrt**-ow-toh-maht of ahn ut loh-**ket**
From the ticket machine or at the counter

Is there a bus to...?	**Is er een bus naar...?** is er un bues nahr...?
Where do I catch the bus to...?	**Waar neem ik de bus naar...?** wahr naym ik du bues nahr...?
We're going to...	**We gaan naar...** wu CHahn nahr...

Where do they sell strippenkaarten?	**Waar verkopen ze strippenkaarten?** wahr ver-**koh**-pu zu **strip**-pu-kahr-tu?
How much is it to...?	**Hoeveel is het naar...?** **hoo**-vayl is ut nahr...?
the centre	**het centrum** ut **sen**-truem
the beach	**het strand** ut strant
the airport	**het vliegveld** ut **vleeCH**-velt
How frequent are the buses to...?	**Hoe vaak gaan er bussen naar...?** hoo vahk CHahn er **bues**-su nahr...?
When is the first/ last bus to...?	**Hoe laat gaat de eerste/ laatste bus naar...?** hoo laht CHaht du **ayr**-stu/ **laht**-stu bues nahr...?
Tell me when I must get off, please	**Zeg me wanneer ik moet uitstappen, alstublieft** zeCH mu wan-**nayr** ik moot **uit**-stap-pu, als-tuu-**bleeft**
I want to get off, please	**Ik wil uitstappen, alstublieft** ik wil **uit**-stap-pu, als-tuu-**bleeft**
This is my stop	**Dit is mijn halte** dit is mein **hal**-tu

YOU MAY HEAR...	
De bus stopt niet in... du bues stopt neet in...	This bus doesn't stop in...
U moet de ... nemen uu moot du ... **nay**-mu	You have to catch the...

Metro

Like other forms of public transport, the metro system in Amsterdam and Rotterdam uses **strippenkaarten** which are valid for 10 journeys or more. Stamp your ticket for the required number of zones when you enter the platform, and hold your stamped ticket to the ticket-reading machine when changing to a different line.

ingang	**in**-CHang	entrance
uitgang	**uit**-CHang	way out/exit

Where is the nearest metro station?

Waar is het dichtstbijzijnde metrostation?
wahr is ut **diCHtst**-bei-zein-du **may**-troh-sta-**shon**?

> **Luggage** (p 88)

How does the (ticket stamping) machine work?	**Hoe werkt de (stempel)automaat?** hoo werkt du (**stem**-pel)ow-toh-maht?
I'm going to...	**Ik ga naar...** ik CHah nahr...
How do I get to...?	**Hoe kom ik in...?** hoo kom ik in...?
Do I have to change?	**Moet ik overstappen?** moot ik **oh**-ver-stap-pu?
Which line goes to...?	**Welke lijn gaat naar...?** **wel**-ku lein CHaht nahr...?
In which direction?	**In welke richting?** In **wel**-ku **riCH**-ting?
What is the next stop?	**Wat is de volgende halte?** wat is du **vol**-CHun-du **hal**-tu?

Train

Trains have two types of compartments: 1st class and 2nd class. All seats are non-smoking. Tickets are bought from ticket machines that take cash and cards. They can also be bought over the counter but a small service charge is payable.

NS en-es **(Nederlandse Spoorwegen)**	Dutch national railways
intercity intercity	intercity
sneltrein **snel**-trein	fast train
stoptrein **stop**-trein	slow train
perron/spoor per-**ron**/spohr	platform
dagretour **daCH** ru-**toor**	day return

FACE TO FACE

A **Hoe laat vertrekt de volgende trein naar...?**
hoo laht ver-**trekt** de **vol**-CHun-du trein nahr...?
When is the next train to...?

B **Om 10:20**
om teen vohr half elf
At 10:20

A **Ik wil graag drie retours, alstublieft**
ik wil CHrahCH drie ru-**toors**, als-tuu-**bleeft**
I'd like three returns, please

B **Dat is dan 36 euro, alstublieft**
dat is dan **zes**-en-der-tiCH eu-**roh**, als-tuu-**bleeft**
That will be 36 euros, please

> **Luggage** (p 88)

Two return tickets to...	**Twee retour naar...** tway ru-**toor** nahr...
A single to...	**Een enkeltje naar...** un **eng**-kel-chu nahr...
1st/2nd class	**Eerste/Tweede klas** **ayr**-stu/**tway**-du klas
Is there a supplement to pay?	**Is er een toeslag?** is er un **too**-slaCH?
When does it arrive in...?	**Hoe laat komt hij aan in...?** hoo laht komt hei ahn in...?
Do I have to change?	**Moet ik overstappen?** moot ik **oh**-ver-stap-pu?
Where?	**Waar?** wahr?
Which platform does it leave from?	**Van welk spoor vertrekt de trein?** van welk spohr ver-**trekt** du trein?
Is this the train for...?	**Gaat deze trein naar...?** CHaht **day**-zu trein nahr...?
When does it leave?	**Hoe laat vertrekt hij?** hoo laht ver-**trekt** hei?
Does the train stop at...?	**Stopt de trein in...?** stopt du trein in...?
Could you let me know when we get to...	**Kunt u mij waarschuwen wanneer wij aankomen in...** kuent uu mei **wahr**-sCHuu-wu wan-**nayr** wei **ahn**-koh-mu in...

Is this seat free?	**Is deze plaats vrij?** is **day**-zu plahts vrei?
Excuse me	**Pardon** par-**don**

YOU MAY HEAR...

De intercity naar ... staat gereed op spoor... du intercity nahr ... staht CHu-**rayt** op spohr...	The intercity train to ... is now ready on platform...

Taxi

I need a taxi	**Ik heb een taxi nodig** ik heb un **tak**-see **noh**-diCH
Where is the taxi rank?	**Waar is de taxistandplaats?** wahr is du **tak**-see-stant-plahts?
Please order me a taxi	**Wilt u alstublieft een taxi bestellen** wilt uu als-tuu-**bleeft** un **tak**-see bu-**stel**-lu
straight away	**direct** dee-**rekt**
for (time)	**voor...** vohr...

How much will a taxi cost to...?	**Hoeveel kost een taxi naar...?** **hoo**-vayl kost un **tak**-see nahr...?
Please take me/ us to...	**Breng mij/ons alstublieft naar...** breng mei/ons als-tuu-**bleeft** nahr...
the station	**het station** ut sta-**shon**
the airport	**het vliegveld** ut **vleeCH**-velt
the centre (of town)	**het centrum** ut **sen**-truem
this address	**dit adres** dit ah-**dres**
I'm in a hurry	**Ik heb haast** ik heb hahst
Is it far?	**Is het ver?** is ut ver?
How much is it?	**Hoeveel is het?** **hoo**-vayl is ut?
That is more than on the meter	**Dat is meer dan op de meter** dat is mayr dan op du **may**-ter
Keep the change	**Laat zo maar zitten** laht zoh mahr **zit**-tu
May I have a receipt, please?	**Mag ik een bonnetje alstublieft?** maCH ik un **bon**-nu-chu als-tuu-**bleeft**?

> **Luggage** (p 88)

Boat and ferry

oversteek **oh**-ver-stayk	crossing
reis reis	journey
cabine kah-**bee**-nu	cabin

When is the next boat/ferry to...? **Wanneer vertrekt de volgende boot/veerboot naar...?**
wan-**nay**r ver-**trekt** du **vol**-CHun-du boht/**vayr**-boht nahr...?

Do you have a timetable? **Heeft u een dienstregeling?**
hayft uu un **deenst**-ray-CHu-ling?

Is there a car ferry to...? **Is er een autoveerboot naar...?**
is er un **ow**-toh-vayr-boht nahr...?

How much is a ticket...? **Hoeveel is een kaartje...?**
hoo-vayl is un **kahr**-chu...?

single **enkel**
eng-kel

return **retour**
ru-**toor**

A day return **Een dagretour**
un daCH-ru-**toor**

How much is the crossing for a car and ... people? **Hoeveel is de oversteek voor een auto en ... personen?**
hoo-vayl is du **oh**-ver-stayk vohr

un **ow**-toh en ... per-**soh**-nu?

How long is the journey?	**Hoe lang duurt de reis?** hoo lang duurt du reis?
What time do we arrive in...?	**Hoe laat komen we aan in...?** hoo laht **koh**-mu wu ahn in...?
When is the first/ last boat?	**Hoe laat is de eerste/laatste boot?** hoo laht is du **ayr**-stu/**laht**-stu

Air travel

Most signs are in Dutch and English and you may go through the airport without having to speak any Dutch.

aankomst **ahn**-komst	arrivals
vertrek ver-**trek**	departures
vlucht vlueCHt	flight
vertraging ver-**trah**-CHing	delay

How do I get to the airport?	**Hoe kom ik op het vliegveld?** hoo kom ik op ut **vleeCH**-velt?
To the airport, please	**Naar het vliegveld, alstublieft** nahr ut **vleeCH**-velt, als-tuu-**bleeft**

How long does it take to get to the airport?	**Hoe lang duurt het om naar het vliegveld te gaan?** hoo lang duurt ut om nahr ut **vleeCH**-velt tu CHahn?
How much is a taxi...?	**hoeveel is een taxi...?** **hoo**-vayl is un tak-**see**...?
into town	**naar de stad** nahr du stat
to the hotel	**naar het hotel** nahr ut hoh-**tel**
Is there a bus or train to the city centre?	**Is er een bus of trein naar het centrum?** is er un bues of trein nahr ut **sen**-truem?
Where is the luggage for the flight from...?	**Waar is de bagage van de vlucht uit...?** wahr is du bah-**CHah**-shu van du vlueCHt uit...?
Where do I check in for the flight to...?	**Waar moet ik inchecken voor de vlucht naar...?** whar moot ik **in**-check-u vohr du vlueCHt nahr...?
My luggage hasn't arrived	**Mijn bagage is niet aangekomen** mein bah-**CHah**-shu is neet **ahn**-CHu-koh-mu

> **Luggage** (p 88)

Customs control

With the Single European Market, European Union (EU) citizens are subject only to spot checks and can go through the blue customs channel (unless they have goods to declare). There is no restriction, either in quantity or value, on goods purchased by travellers in another EU country, provided they are for their own personal use (see the relevant guidelines).

paspoortcontrole **pas**-pohrt-kon-troh-lu	passport control
EU paspoorthouders ay uu **pas**-pohrt-how-ders	EU passport holders
douane doo-**ah**-nu	customs control
niets aan te geven neets ahn tu **CHay**-vu	nothing to declare
aangifte goederen **ahn**-CHif-tu **CHoo**-du-ru	articles to declare

Do I have to pay duty on this?
Moet ik hiervoor invoerrechten betalen?
moot ik **heer**-vohr **in**-voor-reCH-tu be-**tah**-lu?

It is for my own personal use
Het is voor mijn persoonlijk gebruik
ut is vohr mein per-**sohn**-luk CHu-**bruik**

Driving

Car hire

rijbewijs **rei**-bu-weis	driving licence
verzekering ver-**zay**-ku-ring	insurance
achteruit-versnelling aCH-ter-**uit**-ver-**snel**-ling	reverse gear

I want to hire a car	**Ik wil een auto huren** ik wil un **ow**-toh **huu**-ru
for ... days	**voor ... dagen** vohr ... **dah**-CHu
for the weekend	**voor het weekeinde** vohr ut **wayk**-ein-du
How much is it...?	**Hoeveel is het...?** **hoo**-vayl is ut...?
per day	**per dag** per daCH
per week	**per week** per wayk

Is there a charge per kilometre?	**Is er een kilometertoeslag?** is er un **kee**-loh-may-ter-**too**-slaCH?
How much?	**Hoeveel?** **hoo**-vayl?
Is fully comprehensive insurance included in the price?	**Is een all-in verzekering inbegrepen in de prijs?** is un all-in ver-**zay**-ku-ring **in**-bu-CHray-pu in du preis?
Do I have to return the car here?	**Moet ik de auto hier terugbrengen?** moot ik du **ow**-toh heer tu-**rueCH**-breng-u?
By what time?	**Hoe laat?** hoo laht?
I'd like to leave the car in...	**Ik wil de auto laten staan in...** ik wil du **ow**-toh **lah**-tu stahn in...

YOU MAY HEAR...	
Breng de auto met een volle tank terug, alstublieft breng du **ow**-toh met un **vol**-lu tank tu-**rueCH**, als-tuu-**bleeft**	Return the car with a full tank, please

Driving and petrol

Speed limits are usually 120 kilometres per hour on the motorway, 80 or 100 km/h on non-motorways, and 50 in built-up areas (or less in designated areas). There is very limited free parking in most towns.

diesel **dee**-zel	diesel
benzine ben-**zee**-nu	petrol
loodvrij **lohd**-vrei	unleaded

Can I park here?	**Kan ik hier parkeren?** kan ik heer par-**kayr**-ru?
How long for?	**Hoelang?** **hoo**-lang?
Free?	**Gratis?** **CHrah**-tis?
Which junction do I take for...?	**Welke afslag is voor...?** **wel**-ku **af**-slaCH is vohr...?
Is there a petrol station near here?	**Is er een benzinepomp in de buurt?** is er un ben-**zee**-nu-pomp in du buurt?
...euros (worth) of unleaded petrol, please	**...euro loodvrije benzine, alstublieft** ...eu-**roh lohd**-vrei-yu ben-**zee**-nu, als-tuu-**bleeft**

Where is...?	**Waar is...?** wahr is...?
the air line	**de luchtpomp** du **lueCHt**-pomp
the water	**het water** ut **wah**-ter
Can I pay with this credit card?	**Kan ik met deze creditcard betalen?** kan ik met **day**-ze **cre**-dit-card bu-**tah**-lu?

YOU MAY HEAR...

Welke pomp heeft u gebruikt? **wel**-ku pomp hayft uu CHu-**bruikt**?	Which pump did you use?

Breakdown

Can you help me?	**Kunt u me helpen?** kuent uu mu **hel**-pu?
My car has broken down	**Mijn auto is kapot** mein **ow**-toh is kah-**pot**
The car won't start	**De auto wil niet starten** du **ow**-toh wil neet **star**-tu
I've run out of petrol	**Ik heb geen benzine meer** ik heb CHayn ben-**zee**-nu mayr

Can you tow me to the nearest garage?	**Kunt u mij naar de dichtstbijzijnde garage slepen?** kuent uu mei nahr du **diCHtst**-bei-zein-du CHah-**rah**-shu **slay**-pu?
Do you have (spare) parts for a (make of car)?	**Heeft u onderdelen voor...?** hayft uu **on**-der-day-lu vohr...?
The ... doesn't work properly	**De/Het ... werkt niet goed** du/ut ... werkt neet CHoot

Car parts

The ... doesn't work	**De/Het ... werkt niet** du/ut ... werkt neet
The ... don't work	**De ... werken niet** de ... **wer**-ku neet

accelerator	**gaspedaal, het**	**CHas**-pu-dahl
battery	**accu, de**	**ak**-kuu
bonnet	**motorkap, de**	**moh**-tor-kap
brakes	**remmen, de**	**rem**-mu
clutch	**koppeling, de**	**kop**-pu-ling
distributor	**verdeler, de**	ver-**day**-ler
engine	**motor, de**	**moh**-tor

exhaust pipe	**uitlaat, de**	**uit**-laht
fuse	**zekering, de**	**zay**-ku-ring
gears	**versnellingen, de**	ver-**snel**-ling-u
handbrake	**handrem, de**	**hant**-rem
headlights	**koplampen, de**	**kop**-lamp-u
ignition	**ontsteking, de**	ont-**stay**-king
indicator	**richtingaan-wijzer, de**	**riCH**-ting-ahn-wei-zer
radiator	**radiator, de**	rah-dee-**ah**-tor
rear lights	**achterlichten, de**	**aCH**-ter-liCH-tu
seat belt	**autogordel, de**	**ow**-toh-CHor-del
spare wheel	**reservewiel, het**	ru-**ser**-vu-weel
spark plugs	**bougie, de**	**boo**-shee
steering	**stuurinrichting, de**	**stuur**-in-riCH-ting
steering wheel	**stuur, het**	stuur
tyre	**band, de**	band
wheel	**wiel, het**	weel
windscreen wiper	**ruitenwisser, de**	**rui**-tu-wis-ser

Road signs

taxi rank

parking for vehicle shown

parking for car sharers

parking for permit-holders only

priority road

end of priority road

park and ride facility

motorway

district numbers (in traffic areas)

optional cycle path

end of cycle path

built-up area

end of built-up area

pedal cycles and mopeds only

danger

Road signs

Staying somewhere

Hotel (booking)

If you haven't booked your accommodation, check with the local tourist office to see if they have a list of hotels and guesthouses. You can also book accommodation through the Netherlands Board of Tourism website, **www.Holland.com**

FACE TO FACE

A **Ik wil graag een éénpersoons-/tweepersoons-kamer**
ik wil CHrahCH un **ayn**-per-sohns-/**tway**-per-sohns-**kah**-mer
I'd like a single/double room

B **Voor hoeveel nachten?**
vohr **hoo**-vayl **naCH**-tu?
For how many nights?

A **Voor één nacht/... nachten van ... tot...**
vohr ayn naCHt/... **naCH**-tu van ... tot...
For one night/... nights from ... to...

Do you have a room for tonight?	**Heeft u een kamer voor vannacht?**
	hayft uu un **kah**-mer vohr van-**naCHt**?
I'd like a room...	**Ik wil een kamer...**
	ik wil un **kah**-mer...
with bath	**met een bad**
	met un bat
with shower	**met een douche**
	met un doosh
with a double bed	**met een tweepersoonsbed**
	met un **tway**-per-sohns-bet
with an extra bed for a child	**met een extra bed voor een kind**
	met un **ex**-trah bet vohr un kint
How much is it per night/per week?	**Hoeveel kost het per nacht/ per week?**
	hoo-vayl kost ut per naCHt/ per wayk?
Is breakfast included?	**Is het ontbijt inbegrepen?**
	is ut ont-**beit in**-bu-CHray-pu?

YOU MAY HEAR...	
We zijn vol wu zein vol	We're full
Uw naam, alstublieft? uuw nahm, als-tuu-**bleeft**?	Your name, please?
Bevestig alstublieft... bu-**ves**-tiCH als-tuu-**bleeft**...	Please confirm...
per brief per breef	by letter
per fax per fax	by fax

Hotel desk

I booked a room...	**Ik heb een kamer gereserveerd...** ik heb un **kah**-mer CHu-ray-ser-**vayrt**...
in the name of...	**op naam van...** op nahm van...
I'd like to see the room	**Ik wil de kamer graag zien** ik wil du **kah**-mer CHrahCH zeen
Where can I park the car?	**Waar kan ik de auto parkeren?** wahr kan ik du **ow**-toh par-**kayr**-ru?

What time is...?	**Hoe laat is het...?** hoo laht is ut...?
dinner	**diner** dee-**nay**
breakfast	**ontbijt** ont-**beit**
The key for room number...	**De sleutel voor kamer nummer...** du **sleu**-tel vohr **kah**-mer **nuem**-mer...
I'm leaving tomorrow	**Ik vertrek morgen** ik ver-**trek mor**-CHu
Would you prepare the bill	**Wilt u de rekening opmaken** wilt uu du **ray**-ku-ning op-**mah**-ku

Camping

How far is...?	**Hoe ver is...?** hoo ver is...?
the beach	**het strand** ut strant
the wood	**het bos** ut bos

Is there a restaurant on the campsite?	**Is er een restaurant op de camping?** is er un res-toh-**rant** op du **kem**-ping?
Do you have any pitches free?	**Zijn er vrije staanplaatsen?** zein er **vrei**-u **stahn**-plaht-su?
Are there showers?	**Zijn er douches?** zein er **doo**-shes?
Is there hot water/ electricity?	**Is er warm water/ elektriciteit?** is er warm **wah**-ter/ ay-lek-tree-see-**teit**?
We'd like to stay for ... nights	**Wij willen ... nachten blijven** wei **wil**-lu ... **naCH**-tu **blei**-vu
How much is it per night...?	**Hoeveel is het per nacht...?** **hoo**-vayl is ut per naCHt...?
for a tent	**voor een tent** vohr un tent
per person	**per persoon** per per-**sohn**

Self-catering

When you are staying in self-catering accommodation, bear in mind that there are regulations about separating rubbish for recycling purposes.

Who do we contact if there are problems?	**Met wie nemen we contact op als er problemen zijn?** met wee **nay**-mu wu con-**tact** op als er proh-**blay**-mu zein?
How does the heating work?	**Hoe werkt de verwarming?** hoo werkt du ver-**war**-ming?
Is there always hot water?	**Is er altijd heet water?** is er al-**teit** hayt **wah**-ter?
Where is the nearest supermarket?	**Waar is de dichtstbijzijnde supermarkt?** wahr is du **diCHtst**-bei-zein-du **suu**-per-markt?
Where do we leave the rubbish?	**Waar laten we het afval?** wahr **lah**-tu wu ut **af**-val?

> **Sightseeing and tourist office** (p 65)

Shopping

Shopping phrases

Some shops close for lunch, usually from 12.30 to 1.30 pm. Department stores remain open all day. In many towns, shops are closed on Monday morning.

FACE TO FACE

A **Waarmee kan ik u helpen?**
wahr-may kan ik uu **hel**-pu?
How can I help you?

B **Heeft u...?**
hayft uu...?
Do you have...?

A **Jazeker. Alstublieft. Anders nog iets?**
yah-**zay**-ker. als-tuu-**bleeft**. **an**-ders noCH eets?
Certainly. Here you are. Anything else?

I'm looking for a present for...	**Ik zoek een cadeau voor...** ik zook un kah-**doh** voor...
my mother	**mijn moeder** mein **moo**-der
a child	**een kind** un kint
Where do they sell...?	**Waar verkopen ze...?** wahr ver-**koh**-pu zu...?
toys	**speelgoed** **spayl**-CHoot
gifts	**cadeautjes** kah-**doh**-chus
It's too expensive for me	**Het is te duur voor mij** ut is tu duur vohr mei
Have you anything else?	**Heeft u iets anders?** hayft uu eets **an**-ders?
Is there a market?	**Is er een markt?** is er un markt?
On which day?	**Op welke dag?** op **wel**-ku daCH?

Shops

uitverkoop	**uit**-ver-kohp	sale/reductions
open tot...	**oh**-pu tot...	open till...

baker	**bakker**	**bak**-ker
bookshop	**boekhandel**	**book**-han-del
butcher	**slager**	**slah**-CHer
chemist	**drogist**	droh-**CHist**
clothes (women's)	**damesmode**	**dah**-mes-moh-du
clothes (men's)	**herenmode**	**hayr**-ru-moh-du
clothes (children's)	**kinderkleding**	**kin**-der-klay-ding
dry-cleaner	**stomerij**	stoh-mu-**rei**
fishmonger	**vishandel**	**vis**-han-del
florist	**bloemist**	bloo-**mist**
gifts	**cadeaus**	kah-**dohs**
greengrocer	**groenteboer**	**CHroon**-tu-boor
hairdresser	**kapper**	**kap**-per
jeweller	**juwelier**	yuu-wu-**leer**
market	**markt**	markt
pharmacy (dispensing)	**apotheek**	ah-poh-**tayk**
shoe shop	**schoenenwinkel**	**sCHoo**-nu-wing-kel
shop	**winkel**	**wing**-kel
sports shop	**sportzaak**	**sport**-zahk
stationer	**kantoorboek-handel**	kan-**tohr**-book-han-del
supermarket	**supermarkt**	**suu**-per-markt
tobacconist	**sigarenhandel**	see-**CHah**-ru-han-del
toy shop	**speelgoedwinkel**	**spayl**-CHoot-wing-kel

Shopping

Food (general)

biscuits	**koekjes, de**	**kook**-yus
bread	**brood, het**	broht
bread roll	**broodje, het**	**broht**-chu
butter	**boter, de**	**boh**-ter
cheese	**kaas, de**	kahs
chicken	**kip, de**	kip
coffee	**koffie, de**	**kof**-fee
cream	**(slag)room, de**	(**slaCH**)rohm
crisps	**chips, de**	ships
eggs	**eieren, de**	**ei**-yu-ru
ham (cooked)	**gekookte ham, de**	CHu-**kohk**-tu ham
ham (smoked)	**gerookte ham, de**	CHu-**rohk**-tu ham
herbal tea	**kruidenthee, de**	**krui**-du-tay
jam	**jam, de**	shem
margarine	**margarine, de**	mar-CHah-**ree**-nu
marmalade	**marmelade, de**	mar-mu-**lah**-du
milk	**melk, de**	melk
orange juice	**sinaasappelsap, het**	**see**-nahs-ap-pel-sap
rice	**rijst, de**	reist
salt	**zout, het**	zowt
smoked sausage	**rookworst, de**	**rohk**-worst

sugar	**suiker, de**	**sui**-ker
tea	**thee, de**	tay
yoghurt	**yoghurt, de**	**yoh**-CHoort

Food (fruit and veg)

Fruit

apples	**appels, de**	**ap**-pels
apricots	**abrikozen, de**	ab-ree-**koh**-zu
bananas	**bananen, de**	bah-**nah**-nu
cherries	**kersen, de**	**ker**-su
grapefruit	**grapefruit, de**	**CHrayp**-fruit
grapes	**druiven, de**	**drui**-vu
lemon	**citroen, de**	see-**troon**
melon	**meloen, de**	mu-**loon**
nectarines	**nectarines, de**	nek-tah-**ree**-nus
oranges	**sinaasappels, de**	**see**-nahs-ap-pels
peaches	**perziken, de**	**per**-zi-ku
pears	**peren, de**	**payr**-ru
pineapple	**ananas, de**	**ah**-nah-nahs
plums	**pruimen, de**	**prui**-mu
raspberries	**frambozen, de**	fram-**boh**-zu
strawberries	**aardbeien, de**	**ahrd**-bei-yu

Vegetables

asparagus	**asperges, de**	as-**per**-shus
carrots	**wortels, de**	**wor**-tels
cauliflower	**bloemkool, de**	**bloom**-kohl
courgettes	**courgettes, de**	koor-**shet**-tus
cucumber	**komkommer, de**	kom-**kom**-mer
french beans	**sperziebonen, de**	**sper**-zee-boh-nu
garlic	**knoflook, de**	**knof**-lohk
leek	**prei, de**	prei
lettuce	**sla, de**	slah
mushrooms	**champignons, de**	sham-ping-**yons**
onions	**uien, de**	**ui**-yu
peas	**doperwten, de**	**dop**-er-tu
peppers	**paprika, de**	**pah**-pree-kah
potatoes	**aardappels, de**	**ahrd**-ap-pels
spinach	**spinazie, de**	spee-**nah**-zee
tomatoes	**tomaten, de**	toh-**mah**-tu

Clothes

women's sizes		men's suit sizes		shoe sizes			
UK	EU	UK	EU	UK	EU	UK	EU
8	36	36	46	2	35	7	41
10	38	38	48	3	36	8	42
12	40	40	50	4	37	9	43
14	42	42	52	5	38	10	44
16	44	44	54	6	39	11	45
18	46	46	56				

FACE TO FACE

A **Kan ik dit passen?**
kan ik dit **pas**-su?
May I try this on?

B **Natuurlijk. Hier is de paskamer**
nah-**tuur**-luk. heer is du **pas**-kah-mer
Of course. Here is the changing room

A **Heeft u dit in andere kleuren/in maat...?**
hayft uu dit in **an**-du-ru **kleu**-ru/in maht...?
Do you have this in other colours/in size...?

B **Dit is de laatste in deze kleur/deze maat**
dit is du **laht**-stu in **day**-zu kleur/**day**-zu maht
This is the last one in this colour/this size

A **Wat jammer!**
wat **yam**-mer!
What a shame!

a bigger size	**een grotere maat** un **CHroh**-tu-ru maht
a smaller size	**een kleinere maat** un **klei**-nu-ru maht
I'm just looking	**Ik kijk alleen** ik keik al-**layn**
I'll take it	**Ik neem het** ik naym ut

YOU MAY HEAR...	
Welke maat? **wel**-ku maht?	What size?
Past het? past ut?	Does it fit?

Clothes (articles)

blouse	**blouse, de**	bloos
coat	**jas, de**	yas
dress	**jurk, de**	yuerk
jacket	**jasje, het**	**ya**-shu
pyjamas	**pyjama, de**	pee-**yah**-mah
sandals	**sandalen, de**	san-**dah**-lu
shirt	**overhemd, het**	**oh**-ver-hemt
shoes	**schoenen, de**	**sCHoon**-u
shorts	**korte broek, de**	**kor**-tu brook

> **Paying** (p 87)

skirt	**rok, de**	rok
socks	**sokken, de**	**sok**-ku
suit	**kostuum/pak, het**	kos-**tuum**/pak
sweater	**trui, de**	trui
swimsuit	**zwempak, het**	**zwem**-pak
tie	**stropdas, de**	**strop**-das
tights	**panty, de**	**pan**-tee
trousers	**broek, de**	brook
t-shirt	**t-shirt, het**	**tee**-shirt
underpants	**onderbroek, de**	**on**-der-brook
underwear	**ondergoed, het**	**on**-der-CHoot

Maps and guides

Do you have a map of...?
Heeft u een plattegrond van...?
hayft uu un plat-tu-**CHront** van...?

Do you have a guide book/leaflet in English?
Heeft u een gids/brochure in het Engels?
hayft uu un CHits/broh-**shuu**-ru in ut **eng**-els?

Where can I buy an English newspaper?
Waar kan ik een Engelse krant kopen?
wahr kan ik un **eng**-el-su krant **koh**-pu?

Do you have any English newspapers/ books?	**Heeft u Engelse kranten/ boeken?** hayft uu **eng**-el-su **kran**-tu/ **book**-u?

Post office

Main post offices are open Monday to Friday (9 am to 5 pm) and on Saturday mornings.

postkantoor **post**-kan-tohr	post office
postbus **post**-bues	PO box
postzegels **post**-zay-CHels	stamps
brievenbus **bree**-vu-bues	letter box

Is there a post office near here?	**Is er een postkantoor in de buurt?** is er un **post**-kan-tohr in du buurt?

> **Asking the way** (p 25) > **Sightseeing** (p 65)

Can I have stamps for ... postcards to Great Britain? | **Mag ik postzegels voor ... briefkaarten naar Groot Brittannië?**
maCH ik **post**-zay-CHuls vohr ... **breef**-kahr-tu nahr CHroht Brit-**tan**-nee-yu?

by air | **per luchtpost**
per **lueCHt**-post

Photos

Do you have a video tape for this video camera? | **Heeft u een videoband voor deze videocamera?**
hayft uu un **vee**-day-oh-bant voor **day**-zu **vee**-day-oh-kah-mu-rah?

Do you have a battery/memory card for this camera? | **Heeft u batterijen/een geheugenkaart voor deze camera?**
hayft uu **bat**-tu-rei-yu/un CHu-**heu**-CHun-kahrt vohr **day**-zu **kah**-mu-rah?

Leisure

Sightseeing and tourist office

The tourist office is called the **VVV** or **Tourist Information**. They should have information on places to stay (hotels, campsites, etc) and on local events and entertainment.

Where is the tourist office?	**Waar is het VVV kantoor?** wahr is ut vay-vay-vay kan-**tohr**?
What can we visit in the area?	**Wat kunnen we bezoeken?** wat **kuen**-nu wu bu-**zoo**-ku?
Have you any leaflets?	**Heeft u brochures?** hayft uu broh-**shuu**-res?
We'd like to go to...	**Wij willen graag naar...** wei **wil**-lu CHrahCH nahr...
How much does it cost to get in?	**Hoeveel is de entree?** **hoo**-vayl is du on-**tray**?
Is there a reduction for...?	**Is er korting voor...?** is er **kor**-ting vohr...?
children	**kinderen** **kin**-du-ru

> **Maps and guides** (p 62)

students	**studenten**
	stuu-**den**-tu
unemployed	**werklozen**
	werk-loh-zu
senior citizens	**65+ers**
	veif-en-zes-tiCH-**plues**-sers

Entertainment

What is there to do in the evenings?	**Wat is er s'avonds te doen?**
	wat is er **sah**-vonts tu doon?
What events are on this week?	**Welke evenementen zijn er deze week?**
	wel-ku ay-vay-nu-**men**-tu zein er **day**-zu wayk?
Is there anything for children?	**Is er iets voor kinderen?**
	is er eets vohr **kin**-du-ru?
I'd like ... tickets for	**Ik wil graag ... kaartjes voor**
	ik wil CHrahCH ... **kahr**-chus vohr
...adults	**...volwassenen**
	...vol-**was**-su-nu
...children	**...kinderen**
	...**kin**-du-ru

YOU MAY HEAR...

De toegang is ... euro de **too**-CHang is ... eu-**roh**	Entry is ... euro(s)

Leisure/interests

Where can I go...?	**Waar kan ik...?** wahr kan ik...?
fishing	**vissen** **vis**-su
horse-riding	**paardrijden** **pahrt**-rei-du
skating	**schaatsen** **sCHaht**-su
swimming	**zwemmen** **zwem**-mu
How much is it...?	**Hoeveel kost het...?** **hoo**-vayl kost ut...?
per hour	**per uur** per uur
per day	**per dag** per daCH

> **Sport** (p 74) > **Walking** (p 76)

Cycling

You will find excellent places for cycling in the Low Countries. The country is flat and there are cycle paths along most main roads. In the cities, car drivers are used to cyclists, but you must still be careful. There are many special cycle routes in the countryside and organized excursions.

I want to hire a bicycle	**Ik wil een fiets huren** ik wil un feets **huu**-ru
How much is the deposit?	**Hoeveel is de waarborgsom?** **hoo**-vayl is du **wahr**-borCH-som?
Does the bicycle have...?	**Heeft de fiets...?** hayft du feets...?
gears	**versnellingen** ver-**snel**-ling-u
brakes	**remmen** **rem**-mu
lights	**licht** liCHt
back-pedal brakes	**terugtrapremmen** tu-**rueCH**-trap-**rem**-mu
When is the bicycle due back?	**Wanneer moet de fiets terug?** wan-**nayr** moot du feets tu-**rueCH**?

Are there any organized tours/marked routes?	**Zijn er georganiseerde fietstochten/fietsroutes?** zein er CHu-or-CHah-nee-**sayr**-du **feets**-toCH-tu/**feets**-roo-tus?
How long is the tour?	**Hoe lang duurt de tocht?** hoo lang duurt du toCHt?
Where/When does it start?	**Waar/Hoe laat begint het?** wahr/hoo laht be-**CHint** ut?
I have a flat tyre (puncture)	**Ik heb een lekke band** ik heb un **lek**-ku bant
Can you repair it?	**Kunt u hem plakken?** kuent uu hem **plak**-ku?
Do you have a...?	**Heeft u een...?** hayft uu un...?
pump	**fietspomp** **feets**-pomp
repair kit	**reparatieset** ray-pah-**rah**-tsee-set
new tube	**nieuwe binnenband** **nee**-yoo-wu **bin**-nu-bant

YOU MAY HEAR...

Kijk uit! keik uit!	Look out!

Flowers

In the spring the bulb fields between Haarlem and The Hague are in full bloom. The famous gardens at **Keukenhof** are well worth a visit. The main flower growers are found around Aalsmeer, just south of Amsterdam.

I want information on the bulb fields	**Ik wil informatie over de bloembollenvelden** ik wil in-for-**mah**-tsee **oh**-ver du **bloom**-bol-lu-**vel**-du
Are there organized day trips/tours?	**Zijn er georganiseerde dagtochten/rondleidingen?** zein er CHu-or-CHah-nee-**sayr**-du **daCH**-toCH-tu/**ront**-lei-ding-u?
When/Where is the flower festival?	**Wanneer/Waar is het bloemencorso?** wan-**nayr**/wahr is ut **bloo**-mu-cor-soh?
I want bulbs for...	**Ik wil bloembollen voor...** ik wil **bloom**-bol-lu vohr...
tulips	**tulpen** **tuel**-pu
daffodils	**narcissen** nar-**sis**-su

> **Shopping** (p 54)

YOU MAY HEAR...	
Een bos bloemen un bos **bloo**-mu	A bunch of flowers
Een boeket un boo-**ket**	A bouquet

Music

Are there any good concerts on?	**Zijn er goede concerten?** zein er **CHoo**-du kon-**ser**-tu?
Where can I get tickets?	**Waar kan ik kaartjes krijgen?** wahr kan ik **kahr**-chus **krei**-CHu?

Cinema

Foreign films in cinemas are usually shown in the original language with Dutch subtitles.

voorstelling **vohr**-stel-ling	performance
pauze **pow**-zu	interval

Where is the cinema?	**Waar is de bioscoop?** wahr is du bee-os-**kohp**?

When does (name film) start?	**Hoe laat begint...?** hoo laht bu-**CHint**...?
How much are the tickets?	**Hoeveel zijn de kaartjes?** **hoo**-vayl zein du **kahr**-chus?
Two (tickets) for the showing at... (time)	**Twee voor de voorstelling van...** tway vohr du **vohr**-stel-ling van...

YOU MAY HEAR...	
Uitverkocht **uit**-ver-koCHt	Sold out

Theatre/opera

toneelstuk toh-**nayl**-stuek	play
zitplaats **zit**-plahts	seat
garderobe CHar-du-**roh**-bu	cloakroom
pauze **pow**-zu	interval

What's on at the theatre?	**Wat speelt er in het theater?** wat spaylt er in ut tay-**ah**-ter?
How much are the tickets?	**Hoeveel kosten de kaartjes?** **hoo**-vayl **kos**-tu du **kahr**-chus?

I'd like two tickets...	**Ik wil graag twee kaartjes...** ik wil CHrahCH tway **kahr**-chus...
for tonight	**voor vanavond** vohr van-**ah**-vont
for tomorrow night	**voor morgenavond** vohr mor-CHun-**ah**-vont
for the 5th of August	**voor 5 augustus** vohr veif ow-**CHues**-tues
What time does the performance begin/end?	**Hoe laat begint/eindigt de voorstelling?** hoo laht bu-**CHint**/**ein**-diCHt du **vohr**-stel-ling?

Television

afstandsbediening **af**-stants-bu-dee-ning	remote control
nieuws **nee**-yoos	news
kanaal kah-**nahl**	channel
programma proh-**CHram**-mah	programme
tekenfilms **tay**-ken-films	cartoons

Where is the television?	**Waar is de televisie?** wahr is du tay-lu-**vee**-see?
How do you switch it on?	**Hoe gaat hij aan?** hoo CHaht hei ahn?

Could you lower the volume please?	**Kunt u het geluid wat zachter zetten, alstublieft?** kuent uu ut CHu-**luit** wat **zaCH**-ter **zet**-tu, als-tuu-**bleeft**?
May I turn the volume up?	**Mag ik het geluid harder zetten?** maCH ik ut CHu-**luit har**-der **zet**-tu?
What's on the television?	**Wat is er op televisie?** wat is er op tay-lu-**vee**-see?
What time is the news?	**Hoe laat komt het nieuws?** hoo laht komt ut **nee**-yoos?
Do you have any English-language channels?	**Heeft u Engelstalige kanalen?** hayft u **eng**-els-tah-li-CHu kah-**nah**-lu?

Leisure

Sport

Where can I...?	**Waar kan ik...?** wahr kan ik...?
play tennis	**tennissen** **ten**-nis-su
play golf	**golfen** **CHol**-fu
go swimming	**zwemmen** **zwem**-mu

go running	**hardlopen**	
	hart-loh-pu	
skate	**schaatsen**	
	sCHaht-su	
How much is it per hour?	**Hoeveel kost het per uur?**	
	hoo-vayl kost ut per uur?	
Do you have to be a member?	**Moet je lid zijn?**	
	moot yu lit zein?	
Can I hire...?	**Kan ik ... huren?**	
	kan ik ... **huu**-ru?	
skates	**schaatsen**	
	sCHaht-su	
a bicycle	**een fiets**	
	un feets	
rackets	**rackets**	
	ra-**kets**	
golf clubs	**golfclubs**	
	CHolf-clubs	
I like...	**Ik hou van...**	
	ik how van...	
sailing	**zeilen**	
	zei-lu	
surfing	**surfen**	
	sur-fu	
walking	**wandelen**	
	wan-du-lu	

Walking

Are there any guided walks?	**Zijn er wandeltochten met gidsen?** zein er **wan**-del-toCH-tu met **CHit**-su?
Are there any special walking routes?	**Zijn er speciale wandelroutes?** zein er spay-see-**ah**-le **wan**-del-roo-tus?
How many kilometres is the walk?	**Hoeveel kilometer is de wandeling?** **hoo**-vayl **kee**-loh-may-ter is du **wan**-du-ling?
How long will it take?	**Hoe lang duurt het?** hoo lang duurt ut?
Do we need special clothing?	**Hebben we speciale kleding nodig?** **heb**-bu wu spay-see-**ah**-lu **klay**-ding **noh**-diCH?
Should we take...?	**Moeten we ... meenemen?** **moo**-tu wu ... **may**-nay-mu?
water	**water** **wah**-ter
food	**eten** **ay**-tu

waterproofs	**regenkleding** **ray**-CHun-klay-ding
a compass	**een kompas** un kom-**pas**
boots	**laarzen** **lahr**-zu

YOU MAY HEAR...	
Wadlopen **wat**-loh-pu	walking across the mudflats (around the West Frisian islands)

Communications

Telephone and mobile

To phone the Netherlands from the UK, the international code is **00 31** followed by the Dutch area code without the leading zero (e.g. Amsterdam **20**, Rotterdam **10**, The Hague **70**) and the number you require. To phone the UK from the Netherlands, dial **00 44** followed by the UK area code without the leading zero.

telefoonkaart tay-lu-**fohn**-kahrt	phonecard
telefoonboek tay-lu-**fohn**-book	telephone directory
gouden gids **CHow**-du CHits	Yellow Pages
antwoordapparaat **ant**-wohrd-ap-pah-raht	answering machine
gsm CHay-es-em	mobile telephone
sms es-em-es	text message

I want to make a phone call	**Ik wil bellen** ik wil **bel**-lu
I'll call back later/ tomorrow	**Ik bel later/morgen terug** ik bel **lah**-ter/**mor**-CHu tu-**rueCH**
Where can I buy a phonecard?	**Waar kan ik een telefoonkaart kopen?** wahr kan ik un tay-lu-**fohn**-kahrt **koh**-pu?
What is your telephone number?	**Wat is uw telefoonnummer?** wat is uuw tay-lu-**fohn**-**nuem**-mer?
Mr Smit, please	**Meneer Smit, alstublieft** mu-**nayr** Smit, als-tuu-**bleeft**
Extension number...	**Toestelnummer...** **too**-stel-nuem-mer...
Can I speak to...?	**Mag ik...?** maCH ik...?
I would like to speak to...	**Ik wil graag ... spreken** ik wil CHrahCH ... **spray**-ku
This is Jim Brown	**U spreekt met Jim Brown** uu spraykt met Jim Brown
Do you have a mobile?	**Heb je een gsm?** heb yu un CHay-es-em?
My mobile number is...	**Mijn gsm nummer is...** mayn CHay-es-em **nuem**-mer is...
I will text you	**Ik stuur je een sms** ik stuur yu un es-em-es
Can you text me?	**Kun je me sms-en?** kuen yu mu es-em-es-su?

Telephone and mobile

YOU MAY HEAR...	
Hallo hal-**loh**	Hello
Met wie spreek ik? met wee sprayk ik?	Who am I speaking to?
Met wie wilt u spreken? met wee wilt uu **spray**-ku?	Who do you wish to talk to?
Daar spreekt u mee dahr spraykt uu may	Speaking
Een ogenblikje un **oh**-CHu-blik-yu	Just a moment
De lijn is bezet du lein is bu-**zet**	It's engaged
Kunt u later terugbellen? kuent uu l**ah**-ter tu-**rueCH**-bel-lu?	Can you try again later?
Wilt u een boodschap achterlaten? wilt uu un **boht**-sCHap **aCH**-ter-lah-tu?	Do you want to leave a message?
U heeft het verkeerde nummer uu hayft ut ver-**kayr**-du **nuem**-mer	You've got the wrong number

YOU MAY HEAR...	
Spreek alstublieft uw boodschap in na de toon... sprayk als-tuu-**bleeft** uuw **boht**-sCHap in nah du tohn ...	Please leave your message after the tone
Er is nog één (Er zijn nog ...) wachtende voor U er is noCH ayn (er zein noCH ...) **waCH**-tun-du vohr uu	There is one person (There are ... people) waiting before you

Text messaging

I will text you	**Ik zal je teksten** ik zal yu **teks**-tu
Can you text me?	**Kun je me teksten?** kuen yu mu **teks**-tu?

E-mail

An informal way of beginning an e-mail is **Beste...**, ending it with **Groeten** (greetings). For a more formal e-mail, begin with **Geachte...**, and end with **Met vriendelijke groet** (with kind regards).

What is your e-mail address?	**Wat is uw e-mail adres?** wat is uuw **ee**-mayl ah-**dres**?
Do you have a website?	**Heeft u een website?** hayft uu un **web**-site?
How do you spell it?	**Hoe spelt u dat?** hoo spelt uu dat?
All one word	**Eén woord** ayn wohrt
My e-mail address is ...	**Mijn e-mail adres is...** mein **ee**-mayl ah-**dres** is...
Can I send an e-mail?	**Kan ik een e-mail sturen?** kan ik un **ee**-mayl **stuu**-ru?
Did you get my e-mail?	**Heeft u mijn e-mail ontvangen?** hayft uu mein **ee**-mayl ont-**vang**-u?

YOU MAY HEAR...

apenstaartje **ah**-pu-stahr-chu	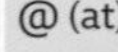 @ (at)

Internet

Are there any internet cafés here?	**Zijn er hier internet cafés?** zein er heer internet ka-**fays**?
How much is it to log on for an hour?	**Hoeveel kost een uur online?** **hoo**-vayl kost un uur online?
I can't log in	**Ik kan niet inloggen** ik kan neet **in**-loCH-CHu

Internet

Fax

To fax the Netherlands from the UK, the code is **00 31** followed by the Dutch area code without the leading zero (e.g. Amsterdam **20**, Rotterdam **10**, The Hague **70**) and then the fax number you require.

Addressing a fax

van	from
ten aanzien van (tav)	for the attention of (fao)
datum	date

Do you have a fax?	**Heeft u een fax?** hayft u un fax?
I want to send a fax	**Ik wil een fax sturen** ik wil un fax **stuu**-ru
What is your fax number?	**Wat is uw faxnummer?** wat is uuw **fax**-nuem-mer?

Practicalities

Money

Banks are generally open from 9 am to 5 pm Monday to Friday. Alternatively, you will find foreign currency exchanges in most cities with extended opening hours. The euro is the currency of The Netherlands. Euro cents are known as **euro centen** (eu-**roh sen**-tu).

Where is the bank?	**Waar is de bank?** wahr is du bank?
Where is the nearest cash machine?	**Waar is de dichtstbijzijnde geldautomaat?** wahr is du **diCHtst**-bei-zein-du **CHelt**-ow-toh-maht?
Where can I change some money?	**Waar kan ik geld wisselen?** wahr kan ik CHelt **wis**-su-lu?
I want to change these traveller's cheques	**Ik wil deze travellercheques wisselen** ik wil **day**-ze **trah**-vel-ler-checks **wis**-su-lu

Money

When does the bank open?	**Wanneer gaat de bank open?** wan-**nayr** CHaht du bank **oh**-pu?
What time does the bank close?	**Hoe laat gaat de bank dicht?** hoo laht CHaht de bank diCHt?
Can I pay with traveller's cheques?	**Kan ik met travellercheques betalen?** kan ik met **trah**-vel-ler-checks be-**tah**-lu?
Can I use my credit card to get euros?	**Kan ik mijn creditcard gebruiken om euros te krijgen?** kan ik mein **cre**-dit-card CHu-**brui**-ku om eu-**rohs** tu **krei**-CHu?
Can I use my card with this cash machine?	**Kan ik mijn pas gebruiken in deze geldautomaat?** kan ik mein pas CHu-**brui**-ku in day-ze **CHelt**-ow-toh-maht?

Paying

How much is it?	**Hoeveel kost het?** **hoo**-vayl kost ut?
Can I pay by debit card? (using a pin code)	**Kan ik pinnen?** kan ik **pin**-nu?
Can I pay by credit card?	**Kan ik betalen per creditcard?** kan ik bu-**tah**-lu per **cre**-dit-card?
Is service included?	**Is de bediening inbegrepen?** is du bu-**dee**-ning **in**-bu-CHray-pu?
Is VAT included?	**Is het inclusief BTW?** is ut in-cluu-**seef** bay-tay-way?
Put it on my bill	**Zet het maar op mijn rekening** zet ut mahr op mein **ray**-ku-ning
I need a receipt	**Ik heb een kassabon nodig** ik heb un **kas**-sah-bon **noh**-diCH
Do I have to pay in advance?	**Moet ik vooruitbetalen?** moot ik vohr-uit-bu-**tah**-lu?
Where do I pay?	**Waar moet ik betalen?** wahr moot ik bu-**tah**-lu?

Luggage

bagage bah-**CHah**-shu	baggage reclaim
bagage depot bah-**CHah**-shu **day**-poh	left-luggage office
gevonden voorwerpen CHu-**von**-du **vohr**-wer-pu	lost property

My luggage hasn't arrived — **Mijn bagage is niet aangekomen**
mein bah-**CHah**-shu is neet **ahn**-CHu-koh-mu

My suitcase has arrived damaged — **Mijn koffer is beschadigd aangekomen**
mein **kof**-fer is bu-**sCHah**-diCHd **ahn**-CHu-koh-mu

> **Train** (p 31) > **Air travel** (p 37)

Repairs

schoenmaker **sCHoon**-mah-ker	shoe repair shop
klaar terwijl u wacht klahr ter-**weil** uu waCHt	repairs while you wait

This is broken — **Het is kapot**
ut is kah-**pot**

Where can I get this repaired? — **Waar kan ik dit laten repareren?**
wahr kan ik dit **lah**-tu ray-pah-**rayr**-ru?

Is it worth repairing? — **Is reparatie de moeite waard?**
is ray-pah-**rah**-tsee du **moo**-yee-tu wahrt?

Repair... — **Repareer...**
ray-pah-**rayr**...

these shoes — **deze schoenen**
day-zu **sCHoo**-nu

my watch — **mijn horloge**
mein hor-**loh**-shu

Laundry

stomerij stoh-mu-**rei**	dry-cleaner
wasserette was-su-**ret**-tu	launderette
zeeppoeder **zayp**-poo-der	washing powder

Is there a launderette near here? — **Is er een wasserette in de buurt?**
is er un was-su-**ret**-tu in du buurt?

Can I borrow an iron? — **Kan ik een strijkijzer lenen?**
kan ik un **streik**-ei-zer **lay**-nu?

Complaints

This doesn't work — **Dit werkt niet**
dit werkt neet

The ... don't work — **De ... werken niet**
du ... **wer**-ku neet

light — **het licht**
ut liCHt

heating — **de verwarming**
du ver-**war**-ming

> **Hotel desk** (p 50)

air conditioning	**de air-conditioning** du **air**-con-di-syoh-ning
It's faulty	**Het is defect** ut is du-**fect**
I want a refund	**Ik wil mijn geld terug** ik wil mein CHelt tu-**rueCH**

Problems

Can you help me?	**Kunt u mij helpen?** kuent uu mei **hel**-pu?
I only speak a little Dutch	**Ik spreek maar een beetje Nederlands** ik sprayk mahr un **bay**-chu **nay**-der-lants
Does anyone here speak English?	**Spreekt hier iemand Engels?** spraykt heer **ee**-mant **eng**-els?
What's the matter?	**Wat is er aan de hand?** wat is er ahn du hant?
I would like to speak to whoever is in charge	**Ik wil graag met de chef spreken** ik wil CHrahCH met du shef **spray**-ku
I'm lost	**Ik ben verdwaald** ik ben ver-**dwahlt**

How do I get to...?	**Hoe kom ik bij...?** hoo kom ik bei...?
I've missed my...	**Ik miste mijn...** ik **mis**-tu mein...
train	**trein** trein
plane	**vliegtuig** **vleeCH**-tuiCH
connection	**verbinding** ver-**bin**-ding
The coach has left without me/us	**De bus is zonder mij/ ons vertrokken** du bues is **zon**-der mei/ ons ver-**trok**-ku
Can you show me how this works?	**Kunt u mij laten zien hoe dit werkt?** kuent uu mei **lah**-tu zeen hoo dit werkt?
I have lost my purse	**Ik heb mijn portemonnaie verloren** ik heb mein por-tu-mon-**nay** ver-**lor**-ru
I need to get to...	**Ik moet naar...** ik moot nahr...
Leave me alone!	**Laat me met rust!** laht mu met ruest!
Go away!	**Ga weg!** CHah weCH!

Emergencies

The Emergency Services telephone number in The Netherlands and Belgium is **112**.

politie poh-**lee**-tsee	police
ambulance am-buu-**lan**-su	ambulance
brandweer **brant**-wayr	fire brigade
ongevallen **on**-CHu-val-lu	casualty department
EHBO ay-hah-bay-oh	first aid (sign)

Help!	**Help!** help!
Fire!	**Brand!** brant!
Can you help me?	**Kunt u mij helpen?** kuent uu mei **hel**-pu?
There's been an accident!	**Er is een ongeluk gebeurd!** er is un **on**-CHu-luek CHu-**beurt**!
Someone is injured	**Er is iemand gewond** er is **ee**-mant CHu-**wont**
Someone has been knocked down by a car	**Er is iemand overreden** er is **ee**-mant oh-ver-**ray**-du
Phone...	**Bel...** bel...

the police	**de politie** du poh-**lee**-tsee
an ambulance	**een ambulance** un am-buu-**lan**-su
please	**alstublieft** als-tuu-**bleeft**
Where is the police station?	**Waar is het politiebureau?** wahr is ut poh-**lee**-tsee-buu-roh?
I want to report a theft	**Ik wil een diefstal aangeven** ik wil un **deef**-stal **ahn**-CHay-vu
I've been robbed/ attacked	**Ik ben beroofd/aangevallen** ik ben be-**rohft**/**aan**-CHu-val-lu
They've stolen my...	**Ze hebben mijn ... gestolen** zu **heb**-bu mein ... CHu-**stoh**-lu
bag	**tas** tas
traveller's cheques	**travellercheques** **trah**-vel-ler-cheks
My car has been broken into	**Er is in mijn auto ingebroken** er is in mein **ow**-toh **in**-CHu-broh-ku
I've been raped	**Ik ben verkracht** ik ben ver-**kraCHt**
I want to speak to a policewoman	**Ik wil met een politie-agente spreken** ik wil met un poh-**lee**-tsee-ah-**CHen**-tu **spray**-ku

I need to make an urgent telephone call	**Ik moet dringend opbellen** ik moot **dring**-unt **op**-bel-lu
I need a report for my insurance	**Ik heb een rapport nodig voor mijn verzekering** ik heb un rap-**port noh**-diCH vohr mein ver-**zay**-ku-ring
My car radio has been stolen	**Mijn autoradio is gestolen** mein **ow**-toh-rah-di-oh is CHu-**stoh**-lu
How much is the fine?	**Hoeveel bedraagt de boete?** **hoo**-vayl bu-**drahCHt** du **boo**-tu?
Where do I pay it?	**Waar moet ik betalen?** wahr moot ik bu-**tah**-lu?
Do I have to pay it straightaway?	**Moet ik het direct betalen?** moot ik ut dee-**rekt** be-**tah**-lu?
I'm very sorry	**Het spijt me heel erg** ut speit mu hayl erCH

YOU MAY HEAR...

U reed door het rode licht uu rayt dohr ut **roh**-du liCHt	You went through a red light
U reed te hard uu rayt tu hart	You were driving too fast

Health

Pharmacy

drogist(erij) droh-**CHist** (droh-CHist-tu-**rei**)	chemist
apotheek ah-poh-**tayk**	pharmacy (dispensing)
dienstdoende apotheek **deenst**-doon-du ah-poh-**tayk**	duty pharmacy

Have you something for...? — **Heeft u iets voor...?** hayft uu eets vohr...?

a headache — **hoofdpijn** **hohft**-pein

car sickness — **reisziekte** **reis**-zeek-tu

diarrhoea — **diarree** dee-ar-**ray**

a sore throat — **keelpijn** **kayl**-pein

I have a rash	**Ik heb een uitslag** ik heb un **uit**-slaCH
Is it safe for children?	**Is het geschikt voor kinderen?** is ut CHu-**sCHikt** vohr **kin**-du-ru?
How much should I take?	**Hoeveel moet ik nemen?** **hoo**-vayl moot ik **nay**-mu?

YOU MAY HEAR...	
Driemaal daags voor/ met/na maaltijden **dree**-mahl dahCHs vohr/ met/nah **mahl**-tei-du	Take it three times a day before/with/ after meals

Words you may need

antiseptic	**antisepticum, het**	an-tee-**sep**-tee-kuem
aspirin	**aspirine, de**	as-pee-**ree**-nu
condoms	**condooms, de**	kon-**dohms**
panty liners	**inlegkruisjes, de**	**in**-leCH-krui-shus
plasters	**pleisters, de**	**pleis**-ters
sanitary towels	**maandverband, het**	**mahnt**-ver-bant
cough	**hoest, de**	hoost
tampons	**tampons, de**	tam-**pons**
toothpaste	**tandpasta, de**	**tant**-pas-tah

Pharmacy

Doctor

In Dutch you can say *either*:

I have a headache	**ik heb hoofdpijn** ik heb **hohft**-pein
or my head hurts	**mijn hoofd doet pijn** mein hohft doot pein

ziekenhuis	**zee**-ku-huis	hospital
ongevallen	**on**-CHu-val-lu	casualty department
spreekuur	**sprayk**-uur	surgery hours

FACE TO FACE

A **Ik voel me ziek**
ik vool mu zeek
I feel ill

B **Heeft u koorts?**
hayft uu kohrts?
Do you have a temperature?

A **Nee. Het doet hier pijn**
nay. ut doot heer pein
No. It hurts here

I need to see a doctor	**Ik moet naar de dokter** ik moot nahr du **dok**-ter
My son/daughter is ill	**Mijn zoon/dochter is ziek** mein zohn/**doCH**-ter is zeek

He/She has a temperature	**Hij/Zij heeft koorts** hei/zei hayft kohrts
I'm diabetic	**Ik heb suikerziekte** ik heb **sui**-ker-zeek-tu
I'm pregnant	**Ik ben in verwachting** ik ben in ver-**waCH**-ting
I'm on the pill	**Ik gebruik de pil** ik CHu-**bruik** du pil
I'm allergic to penicillin	**Ik ben allergisch voor penicilline** ik ben al-**ler**-CHees voor pay-ni-si-**lee**-nu
Will he/she have to go to hospital?	**Moet hij/zij naar het ziekenhuis?** moot hei/zei nahr ut **zee**-ku-huis?
Will I have to pay?	**Moet ik betalen?** moot ik bu-**tah**-lu?
How much will it cost?	**Hoeveel kost het?** **hoo**-vayl kost ut?
I need a receipt for the insurance	**Ik heb een ontvangstbewijs nodig voor de verzekering** ik heb un ont-**vangst**-bu-weis **noh**-diCH vohr du ver-**zay**-ku-ring

YOU MAY HEAR...

Het is niet ernstig ut is neet **ern**-stiCH	It's not serious

Dentist

I need a dentist	**Ik heb een tandarts nodig** ik heb un **tant**-arts **noh**-diCH
He/She has toothache	**Hij/Zij heeft kiespijn** hei/zei hayft **kees**-pein
Can you do a temporary filling?	**Kunt u een tijdelijke vulling maken?** kuent uu un **tei**-du-lu-ku **vuel**-ling **mah**-ku?
It hurts (me)	**Het doet pijn** ut doot pein
Can you give me something for the pain?	**Kunt u mij iets tegen de pijn geven?** kuent uu mei eets **tay**-CHu du pein **CHay**-vu?
I think I have an abscess	**Ik geloof dat ik een abces heb** ik CHu-**lohf** dat ik un **ab**-ses heb
Can you repair my dentures?	**Kunt u mijn kunstgebit repareren?** kuent uu mein **kuenst**-CHu-bit ray-pah-**rayr**-ru?
Do I have to pay?	**Moet ik betalen?** moot ik bu-**tah**-lu?
How much will it be?	**Hoeveel kost het?** **hoo**-vayl kost ut?

> **Emergencies** (p 93)

I need a receipt for my insurance	**Ik heb een ontvangstbewijs nodig voor mijn verzekering** ik heb un ont-**vangst**-bu-weis **noh**-diCH vohr mein ver-**zay**-ku-ring

YOU MAY HEAR...	
Hij moet er uit hei moot er uit	It has to come out
Ik ga u een injectie geven ik CHah uu un in-**yek**-tsee **CHay**-vu	I'm going to give you an injection

Different types of travellers

Disabled travellers

All public buildings, including museums, have facilities for disabled visitors. It is best to check accessibility before visiting other tourist attractions.

What facilities do you have for disabled people?	**Welke faciliteiten heeft u voor invaliden?** **wel**-ku fah-see-lee-**tei**-tu hayft uu vohr in-vah-**lee**-du?
Are there any toilets for the disabled?	**Zijn er toiletten voor invaliden?** zein er twa-**let**-tu vohr in-vah-**lee**-du?
Do you have any bedrooms on the ground floor?	**Heeft u slaapkamers op de begane grond?** hayft uu **slahp**-kah-mers op du bu-**CHa**-nu CHront?
Is there a lift?	**Is er een lift?** is er un lift?

Where is the lift?	**Waar is de lift?** wahr is du lift?
Are there any ramps?	**Zijn er hellende opritten?** zein er **hel**-lun-du **op**-rit-tu?
How many stairs are there?	**Hoeveel trappen zijn er?** **hoo**-vayl **trap**-pu zein er?
How wide is the entrance door?	**Hoe breed is de ingang?** hoe brayt is du **in**-CHang?
Where is the wheelchair-accessible entrance?	**Waar is de ingang voor rolstoelen?** wahr is du **in**-CHang vohr **rol**-stoo-lu?
Is there a reduction for handicapped people?	**Is er korting voor gehandicapten?** is er **kor**-ting vohr CHu-**hen**-dee-cap-tu?
Is there somewhere I can sit down?	**Kan ik ergens zitten?** kan ik **er**-CHuns **zit**-tu?

With kids

Very young children may travel free on public transport, and discounts are usually available for older children. This also applies to attractions such as museums.

A child's ticket	**Een kinderkaartje** un **kin**-der-kahr-chu
He/She is ... years old	**Hij/Zij is ... jaar** hei/zei is ... yahr
Is there a reduction for children?	**Krijgen kinderen korting?** **krei**-CHu **kin**-du-ru **kor**-ting?
Do you have a children's menu?	**Heeft u een kindermenu?** hayft uu un **kin**-der-mu-nuu?
Do you have...	**Heeft u...** hayft uu...
a high chair	**een kinderstoel** un **kin**-der-stool
a cot	**een wieg** un weeCH
I have two children	**ik heb twee kinderen** ik heb tway **kin**-du-ru
He/She is 10 years old	**Hij/Zij is tien jaar** hei/zei is teen yahr
Do you have any children?	**Heeft u kinderen?** hayft uu **kin**-du-ru?

> **Pharmacy** (p 96) > **Doctor** (p 98)

Reference

Alphabet

Below are the words used for clarification when spelling something out.

Hoe spel je het? hoo spel yu ut?	How do you spell it?
A van Amsterdam, B van bravo ah van am-ster-**dam**, bay van **brah**-voh	A for Amsterdam, B for Bravo

A	ah	**Amsterdam**	am-ster-**dam**
B	bay	**Bravo**	**brah**-voh
C	say	**Charlie**	**char**-lee
D	day	**Dirk**	dirk
E	ay	**Edam**	**ay**-dam
F	ef	**Freddie**	**fred**-dee
G	CHay	**goed**	CHoot

H	hah	**help**	help
I	ee	**Isaac**	**ee**-sahk
J	yay	**Jaap**	yahp
K	kah	**kilo**	**kee**-loh
L	el	**lasso**	las-**soh**
M	em	**moeder**	**moo**-der
N	en	**Nico**	**nee**-koh
O	oh	**Otto**	**ot**-toh
P	pay	**paard**	pahrt
Q	kuu	**Quaker**	**kway**-ker
R	er	**Rudolf**	**ruu**-dolf
S	es	**suiker**	**sui**-ker
T	tay	**tafel**	**tah**-fel
U	uu	**uur**	uur
V	vay	**vogel**	**voh**-CHel
W	way	**wind**	wint
X	iks	**xylofoon**	see-loh-**fohn**
Y	ei	**Yankee**	**yang**-kee
Z	zet	**zout**	zowt

YOU MAY HEAR...

IJ (lange ij) ei (**lang**-u ei)

Reference

Measurements and quantities

The metric system is used. Note that a Dutch pound – **pond** is 500 grams, and the Dutch ounce – **ons** is 100 grams.

Liquids

1/2 litre of...	**halve liter...**	**hal**-vu **lee**-ter...
a litre of...	**een liter...**	un **lee**-ter...
a bottle of...	**een fles...**	un fles...
a glass of...	**een glas...**	un CHlas...

Weights

100 grams of...	**een ons...**	un ons...
1/2 kilo of... (500 g)	**een pond...**	un pont...
a kilo of... (1000 g)	**een kilo...**	un **kee**-loh...

Food

a slice of...	**een plak...**	un plak...
a portion of...	**een portie...**	un **por**-tsee...
a dozen...	**een dozijn...**	un doh-**zein**...
a box of...	**een doos...**	un dohs...
a packet of... (large)	**een pak...**	un pak...
a packet of... (small)	**een pakje...**	un **pak**-yu...
a tin of...	**een blik...**	un blik...
a jar of...	**een pot...**	un pot...

Miscellaneous

a quarter	**een kwart**	un kwart
ten per cent	**tien procent**	teen proh-**sent**
more...	**meer...**	mayr...
less...	**minder...**	**min**-der...
enough	**genoeg**	CHu-**nooCH**
double	**dubbel**	**dueb**-bel
twice	**twee keer**	tway kayr
three times	**drie keer**	dree kayr

Numbers

0 **nul** nuel
1 **één** ayn
2 **twee** tway
3 **drie** dree
4 **vier** veer
5 **vijf** veif
6 **zes** zes
7 **zeven** **zay**-vu
8 **acht** aCHt
9 **negen** **nay**-CHu
10 **tien** teen
11 **elf** elf
12 **twaalf** twahlf
13 **dertien** **der**-teen
14 **veertien** **vayr**-teen
15 **vijftien** **veif**-teen
16 **zestien** **zes**-teen
17 **zeventien** **zay**-vu-teen
18 **achttien** **aCHt**-teen
19 **negentien** **nay**-CHu-teen
20 **twintig** **twin**-tiCH
21 **éénentwintig** **ayn**-en-twin-tiCH
22 **tweeëntwintig** **tway**-en-twin-tiCH
23 **drieëntwintig** **dree**-en-twin-tiCH
24 **vierentwintig** **veer**-en-twin-tiCH

25	**vijfentwintig veif**-en-twin-tiCH
30	**dertig der**-tiCH
40	**veertig vayr**-tiCH
50	**vijftig veif**-tiCH
60	**zestig zes**-tiCH
70	**zeventig zay**-vun-tiCH
80	**tachtig taCH**-tiCH
90	**negentig nay**-CHun-tiCH
100	**honderd hon**-dert
110	**honderdtien hon**-dert-teen
500	**vijfhonderd veif**-hon-dert
1,000	**duizend dui**-zunt
2,000	**tweeduizend tway**-dui-zunt
1 million	**één miljoen** ayn mil-**yoon**

1st **eerste**
ayr-stu

2nd **tweede**
tway-du

3rd **derde**
der-du

4th **vierde**
veer-du

5th **vijfde**
veif-du

Days and months

Dutch names of days of the week and months are written without a capital letter.

Days

Monday	**maandag**	**mahn**-daCH
Tuesday	**dinsdag**	**dins**-daCH
Wednesday	**woensdag**	**woons**-daCH
Thursday	**donderdag**	**don**-der-daCH
Friday	**vrijdag**	**vrei**-daCH
Saturday	**zaterdag**	**zah**-ter-daCH
Sunday	**zondag**	**zon**-daCH

Months

January	**januari**	yah-nuu-**ah**-ree
February	**februari**	fay-bruu-**ah**-ree
March	**maart**	mahrt
April	**april**	ap-**ril**
May	**mei**	mei
June	**juni**	**yuu**-nee
July	**juli**	**yuu**-lee
August	**augustus**	**ow**-CHues-tues
September	**september**	sep-**tem**-ber

October	**oktober**	ok-**toh**-ber
November	**november**	noh-**vem**-ber
December	**december**	day-**sem**-ber

What's the date?	**Wat is de datum?** wat is du **dah**-tuem?
What day is it today?	**Welke dag is het vandaag?** **wel**-ku daCH is ut van-**dahCH**?
It's the 5th of August 2007	**Het is 5 augustus 2007** ut is veif ow-**CHues**-tues **tway**-dui-zent-**zay**-vu
on Saturday	**op zaterdag** op **zah**-ter-daCH
on Saturdays	**'s zaterdags** s-**zah**-ter-daCHs
every Saturday	**iedere zaterdag** **ee**-du-ru **zah**-ter-daCH
this Saturday	**deze zaterdag** **day**-zu **zah**-ter-daCH
next/last Saturday	**volgende/vorige zaterdag** **vol**-CHun-du/**vor**-ri-CHu **zah**-ter-daCH
in June	**in juni** in **yuu**-nee
at the beginning/ end of June	**begin/eind juni** bu-**CHin**/eint **yuu**-nee
before summer	**voor de zomer** vohr du **zoh**-mer

Reference

during the summer **tijdens de zomer**
tei-dens du **zoh**-mer
after the summer **na de zomer**
nah du **zoh**-mer

Time

In principle, the 24-hour clock is used. However, after **12.00** midday, the Dutch speak of **13.00 - één uur**, **14.00 - twee uur**, etc. Formal announcements, such as in railway stations, and written notices use the 24-hour clock consistently (**13.00 - dertien uur**, **14.00 - veertien uur**, etc.).

Note that 9.30 is **half tien**, literally meaning 'half ten', 9.20 is **tien voor half tien**, literally 'ten minutes before half ten', and so on.

What time is it? **Hoe laat is het?**
hoo laht is ut?
am **voormiddag**
vohr-mid-daCH
pm **namiddag**
nah-mid-daCH
It's... **Het is...**
ut is...

2 o'clock	**2 uur** tway uur
3 o'clock	**3 uur** dree uur
6 o'clock (etc.)	**6 uur** zes uur
It's 1 o'clock	**Het is 1 uur** ut is ayn uur
It's 12.00 midday	**het is 12 uur 's middags** ut is twahlf uur **smid**-daCHs
At midnight	**Middernacht** mid-der-**naCHt**
9	**9 uur** **nay**-CHu uur
9.10	**10 over 9** teen **oh**-ver **nay**-CHu
quarter past 9	**kwart over 9** kwart **oh**-ver **nay**-CHu
9.20	**10 voor half 10** teen vohr half teen
9.30	**half 10** half teen
9.35	**5 over half 10** veif **oh**-ver half teen
9.40	**10 over half 10** teen **oh**-ver half teen

quarter to 10	**kwart voor 10** kwart vohr teen
10 to 10	**10 voor 10** teen vohr teen

Time phrases

When does it open?	**Hoe laat gaat het open?** hoo laht CHaht ut **oh**-pu?
When does it close?	**Hoe laat gaat het dicht?** hoo laht CHaht ut diCHt?
When does it begin?	**Hoe laat begint het?** hoo laht bu-**CHint** ut?
When does it finish?	**Hoe laat eindigt het?** hoo laht **ein**-diCHt ut?
at 3 o'clock	**om 3 uur** om dree uur
before 3 o'clock	**voor 3 uur** vohr dree uur
after 3 o'clock	**na 3 uur** nah dree uur
today	**vandaag** **van**-dahCH
tonight	**vanavond** van-**ah**-vont

tomorrow	**morgen** **mor**-CHu
yesterday	**gisteren** **CHis**-tu-ru
this morning	**vanmorgen** van-**mor**-CHu
this afternoon	**vanmiddag** van-**mid**-daCH
this evening	**vanavond** van-**ah**-vont
at half past 7	**om half 8** om half aCHt
at about 10 o'clock	**om ongeveer 10 uur** om on-CHu-**vayr** teen uur

Eating out

Eating places

Bar/Café Serves drinks, coffee, tea and snacks.

Snackbar Like a fish and chip shop, but usually without the fish.

Cafetaria More sophisticated than a snackbar, but not like a restaurant, usually self-service.

Pannenkoekhuis Pancake house. A popular eating place offering an amazing variety of pancakes.

Grand café Serves drinks, coffee, tea and snacks, but also lunch and dinner.

Eetcafé Pub which serves meals in the evening, but with less choice than a restaurant.

Restaurant In restaurants lunch is usually served between 12.30 and 2.30 pm. Dinner starts at 6 and usually goes on until 9.30 or 10 pm.

Broodjeswinkel Sandwich shop.

In a bar/café

If you want black coffee ask for **zwarte koffie**. For a white coffee ask for **koffie met melk**. Lager is called **bier** or **pils** and is served with a head of foam.

FACE TO FACE

A **Wat wilt u?**
wat wilt uu?
What would you like?

B **Een warme chocolademelk met slagroom, alstublieft**
un **war**-mu shoh-koh-**lah**-du-melk met **slaCH**-rohm, als-tuu-**bleeft**
A hot chocolate with whipped cream, please

a coffee	**een koffie** un **kof**-fee
a lager	**een pils** un pils

Eating out

a glass of white wine	**een glaas witte wijn** un CHlas **wit**-tu wein
...please	**...alstublieft** ...als-tuu-**bleeft**
a tea...	**een thee...** un tay...
with milk/lemon	**met melk/citroen** met melk/see-**troon**
no sugar	**zonder suiker** **zon**-der **sui**-ker
for me	**voor mij** vohr mei
for him/her/us	**voor hem/haar/ons** vohr hem/hahr/ons
with ice, please	**met ijs, alstublieft** met eis, als-tuu-**bleeft**
A bottle of mineral water	**Een fles mineraalwater** un fles mee-nu-**rahl**-wah-ter
sparkling	**met prik** met prik
still	**zonder prik** **zon**-der prik

Other drinks to try

advocaat Dutch liqueur based on egg yolks
jenever Dutch gin: **jonge** young, **oude** old
abdijbier/Trappist traditional, often strong, beer brewed in (Trappist) monasteries

Reading the menu

Most restaurants have a menu displayed next to the entrance. Inside there may be a board with specials and the dish or menu of the day.

YOU MAY HEAR...	
Dagschotel **daCH**-sCHoh-tel	Dish of the day
Menu van de dag mu-**nuu** van de daCH	Menu of the day (set menu)

Menu	Menu
Voorgerechten	Starters
Soep	Soups
Salades	Salads
Vlees	Meat
Vis	Fish
Eigerechten	Egg dishes
Pasta	Pasta
Rijstschotels	Rice dishes
Kaas	Cheese
Nagerechten	Dessert
Dranken	Drinks
Bediening inbegrepen	Service included

In a restaurant

Dutch home cooking tends to be simple, wholesome and filling. Hence you will find few restaurants specialising in Dutch cuisine.

FACE TO FACE

A **Ik wil een tafel reserveren voor ... personen**
ik wil un **tah**-fel ray-ser-**vayr**-ru vohr ... per-**soh**-nu
I'd like to book a table for ... people

B **Voor wanneer?**
vohr wan-**nayr**?
When for?

A **Voor vanavond/voor morgenavond ... om half negen**
vohr van-**ah**-vont/vohr mor-CHun-**ah**-vont ... om half **nay**-CHu
for tonight/for tomorrow night ... at 8:30 pm

The menu, please	**Het menu, alstublieft** ut mu-**nuu**, als-tuu-**bleeft**
What is the dish of the day?	**Wat is de dagschotel?** wat is du **daCH**-sCHoh-tel?
Do you have...?	**Heeft u...?** hayft u...?
à la carte menu	**een à la carte menu** un ah lah kart mu-**nuu**

a children's menu	**een kindermenu** un **kin**-der-mu-nuu
What can you recommend?	**Wat kunt u aanbevelen?** wat kuent uu **ahn**-bu-vay-lu?
What is this?	**Wat is dit?** wat is dit?
I'll have this	**Ik wil dit** ik wil dit
Excuse me!	**Pardon!** par-**don**!
More bread/more water, please	**Meer brood/meer water, alstublieft** mayr broht/mayr **wah**-ter, als-tuu-**bleeft**
another bottle	**nog een fles** noCH un fles
the bill	**de rekening** du **ray**-ku-ning
Is service included?	**Is de bediening inbegrepen?** is du bu-**dee**-ning **in**-bu-CHray-pu?

Vegetarian

Most restaurants will have vegetarian dishes. In addition there are vegetarian and healthfood restaurants serving food without chemical additives. Be aware that many soups, even vegetable soup, may contain meatballs (**gehaktballen**).

Are there any vegetarian restaurants here?	**Zijn er hier vegetarische restaurants?** zein er heer vay-CHu-**tah**-ree-su res-toe-**rants**?
Do you have any vegetarian dishes?	**Heeft u vegetarische gerechten?** hayft uu vay-CHu-**tah**-ree-su CHu-**reCH**-tu?
Which dishes have no meat/fish?	**Welke gerechten bevatten geen vlees/vis?** **wel**-ku CHu-**reCH**-tu bu-**vat**-tu CHayn vlays/vis?
What fish dishes do you have?	**Wat voor visgerechten heeft u?** wat vohr vis-CHu-**reCH**-tu hayft uu?
I don't like meat	**Ik hou niet van vlees** ik how neet van vlays

What do you recommend?	**Wat kunt u aanbevelen?** wat kuent uu **ahn**-bu-vay-lu?
Is it made with vegetable stock?	**Is het gemaakt met vegetarische bouillon?** is ut CHu-**mahkt** met vay-CHu-**tah**-ree-su bool-**yon**?
Which dishes contain...?	**Welke gerechten bevatten...?** wel-ku CHu-**reCH**-tu bu-**vat**-tu...?
milk	**melk** melk
butter	**boter** **boh**-ter
cheese	**kaas** kahs
eggs	**eieren** **ei**-yu-ru
gluten	**gluten** **CHluu**-tun
chemical additives	**chemische toevoegingen** **CHay**-mee-su **too**-voo-CHing-u

Menu reader

Everyday words which are the same in Dutch and English have not been included.

aalbessen redcurrants
aardappel potato
aardappel in de schil gekookt jacket potato
aardappelpuree mashed potato
aardbei strawberry
abrikoos apricot
advocaat advocaat (egg-based liqueur)
alcoholvrije non-alcoholic
amandel almond
ananas pineapple
ananassap pineapple juice
andijvie stamppot mashed potato and endive
anijs aniseed
aperitief aperitif
appel apple
appelbeignet apple fritter
appelbol apple dumpling
appelflap apple pastry
appelgebak apple cake
appelmoes apple sauce

appeltaart apple tart
artisjokken artichokes
asperge (punten) asparagus (tips)
aspergesoep asparagus soup
Atjar tjampoer pickled vegetables (Indonesian)
augurk gherkin
avondeten dinner
azijn vinegar

baars perch
Babi pangang grilled sweet-and-sour pork (Indonesian)
balletjessoep beef or chicken soup with meatballs
Bami goreng special fried noodles (Indonesian)
banaan banana
basilicum basil
bediening service
bediening inbegrepen service included
Belgische wafels Belgian waffles
berenburg Frisian gin
beschuit round rusk-type biscuits
bessenjenever blackcurrant gin
biefstuk beef steak
  niet gaar/rood rare
  net gaar gebakken medium
  doorgebakken well-done
bier beer
  donker dark
  licht/blond lager

bier van het vat draught beer
bieslook chives
bieten beetroot
bijgerechten side dishes
bisschopswijn mulled wine
bitterballen deep-fried breaded meat balls served as a snack
bitterkoekjes almond biscuits
bittertje bitter aperitif
blinde vinken minced meat rolled in sliced veal
bloedworst black pudding
bloemkool cauliflower
boerenjongens raisins soaked in brandy
boerenkool curly kale
boerenmeisjes apricots soaked in brandy
boerenomelet vegetable and bacon omelette
bokking kipper
bonen beans
bonenkruid savoury (herb)
borrel 'shot' of spirit
borrelhapje bar snack
borststuk breast
bosbessen blueberries
bot flounder or bone
boter butter
boterham sandwich
boterkoek shortbread
botersaus butter sauce
bouillon broth

braadhaantje spring chicken
braadworst frying sausage
braam blackberry
brandewijn brandy
brasem bream
brood bread
  krentenbrood currant bread
  roggebrood rye bread
  volkorenbrood wholemeal bread
  witbrood white bread
broodmaaltijd bread and cheese, cold meat, eggs, jam and pickles
broodje bread roll or bun
  broodje gezond (healthy) salad roll
  broodje kaas cheese roll
broodjeswinkel sandwich shop
brut very dry
BTW en bediening inbegrepen VAT and service charge included

café café
cafeïnevrij decaffeinated coffee
cafetaria snack bar
caramel pudding crème caramel
cassis blackcurrant liqueur or soft drink
champignon mushroom
chipolatapudding egg pudding with biscuits and liqueur
chips crisps

chocola(de) chocolate
reep chocolade chocolate bar
chocolademelk chocolate milk drink
citroen lemon
citroenbrandewijn lemon brandy
citroenjenever lemon gin
citroentje met suiker brandy with lemon and sugar
cornflakes cereal
croissanterie French bread and croissant shop

dadel date
dagschotel dish of the day
dame blanche vanilla ice-cream with hot chocolate sauce
dille dill
diner dinner
donker bier dark beer
doorgebakken well-done
doperwtjes peas
dragon tarragon
drank(jes) drink(s)
droog dry
drop liquorice sweets
druif grape
blauwe black grape
witte white grape
druivensap grape juice
duif pigeon
Duitse biefstuk minced-beef steak

Edam medium-hard cheese in a distinctive coat of red wax
eend duck
ei egg
gepocheerd ei poached egg
gevulde eieren stuffed eggs
hardgekookt ei hardboiled egg
roerei scrambled egg
spiegeleieren fried eggs
eiersalade egg mayonnaise
eigengemaakt homemade
entrecôte ribeye steak
erwt pea
erwtensoep met kluif pea soup with pork and sausage
exclusief not included

fazant pheasant
filet fillet
filet américain steak tartare
flensje thin pancake
fles bottle
halve fles half bottle
Foe yong hai leek, prawn and onion omelette with sweet-and-sour sauce (Indonesian)
forel trout
forel à la meunière trout with lemon and parsley
framboos raspberry
Franse uiensoep French onion soup

Friese nagelkaas clove-flavoured cheese
frikandel meatball, rissole
frisdrank soft drink
frites chips
fruit naar keuze a choice of fruit

gaar well done
Gado gado vegetables in peanut sauce (Indonesian)
gans goose
garnalen prawns
gebak individual cake/pastry
gebakken fried
gebonden soep cream soup
gebraden roasted
gefrituurd deep fried
gegrild grilled or broiled
gehakt minced
gehaktbal meatball
gekoeld iced
gekookt boiled
gekruid seasoned
gemarineerd marinated
gember ginger
gemberbier ginger ale
gemberkoek gingerbread or cake
gemengd mixed
gepaneerd breaded
gepocheerd ei poached egg
geraspt grated

gerecht dish or course
gerookt smoked
geroosterd grilled
geroosterd brood toast
gesmolten boter clarified butter
gesmoord braised
gestoofd stewed
gestoomd steamed
Geuzelambiek Flemish wheat beer
gevarieerde assorted
gevogelte poultry
gevuld stuffed
gezouten salted
gin-tonic gin and tonic
glas glass
  glaasje small glass
  groot glas large glass
Goudakaas medium-hard cheese, similar to Edam
grapefruitsap grapefruit juice
griet brill
groente vegetable

Haagse bluf egg-white dessert with redcurrant sauce
haantje cockerel
haas hare
hachee spiced mincemeat
half, halve half
  halve fles half bottle

ham ham
hardgekookt ei hardboiled egg
haring herring
nieuwe salt-cured
haringsalade herring salad with apple, pickles, potato, beetroot and mayonnaise
hart heart
havermoutpap porridge
hazelnoot hazelnut
hazepeper jugged hare
heilbot halibut
heldere soep consommé
Hollandse nieuwe salt-cured herring with onions
Hollandse saus Hollandaise sauce
honing honey
hoofdgerecht main course
houtsnip woodcock
huiswijn house wine
hutspot mashed potato and vegetables with fried sausages
huttenkaas cottage cheese
huzarensalade potato salad with apple, pickles and ham

ijs ice or ice-cream
aardbeien strawberry
chocolade chocolate
pistache pistachio
vanille vanilla

ijstaart ice-cream cake
ijsthee iced tea
inclusief included
Indonesische gerechten Indonesian dishes

jachtschotel game and potato casserole served with apple sauce
jagersaus rich wine sauce
jam jam
jenever gin
jonge jenever young gin
jonge kaas fresh cheese
jus gravy

kaas cheese
kaassaus cheese sauce
kabeljauw cod
kalfsborst veal breast
kalfshaas veal tenderloin
kalfskotelet veal cutlet
kalfsoester thin veal fillet
kalfstong veal tongue
kalfsvlees veal
kalkoen turkey
kaneel cinnamon
kappertjes capers
kappertjessaus butter sauce with capers
kapucijners marrowfat peas
karaf carafe

karbonade chop or cutlet
karnemelk buttermilk
karper carp
kastanjes chestnuts
kastanjepuree chestnut purée
kaviaar caviar
kerrie curry
kers cherry
zwarte kersen black cherries
kersenbrandewijn kirsch
kervelsoep chervil soup
kilo kilo
halve kilo half a kilo
kindermenu children's menu
kip chicken
gebraden kip roast chicken
kipfilet *or* **kippenborst** chicken breast
kippenbout chicken leg
kippenlevertjes chicken liver
knakworst frankfurter
knoflook garlic
knolselderij celeriac
koek cake
koekje biscuit
koffie coffee
cafeïnevrije decaffeinated coffee
koffie met melk white coffee
koffie met room coffee with cream
koffie met slagroom coffee with whipped cream

koffie verkeerd coffee and a lot of hot milk
potje koffie pot of coffee
zwarte koffie black coffee
koffiebroodjes sweet buns or pastries
koffieshop coffeeshop
koffietafel a light lunch of bread and butter with assorted toppings, and coffee
kokosnoot coconut
komijnekaas cheese with cumin seeds
komkommer cucumber
konijn rabbit
koninginnensoep cream of chicken soup
kool cabbage
kopje cup
kotelet chop or cutlet
koud cold
koud vlees cold meat
krab crab
kreeft lobster
krent currant
krentenbrood currant bread
Kriek Belgian cherry beer
kroepoek prawn crackers
kroket croquette
kruiden seasoning or herbs
kruidenthee herbal tea
kruidnagel clove
kruisbes gooseberry
kuiken spring chicken

kummel caraway seeds
kunstmatige zoetstof artificial sweetener
kwark fresh white, very mild cheese
kwarktaart cheesecake
kwartel quail

lamsbout leg of lamb
lamskotelet lamb cutlet
lamsvlees lamb
laurier bay leaf
lekkerbekje deep-fried haddock or plaice
lendestuk sirloin
lever liver
leverworst/leverkaas liver sausage
licht light
  licht bier lager
likeur liqueur
Limburgse kaas spicy cream cheese
limonade lemonade
linzen lentils
liter litre
loempia spring roll (Indonesian)

maïs corn
maïskolf corn on the cob
makreel mackerel
mandarijn mandarin
marmelade marmalade
marsepein marzipan

meel flour
melk milk
meloen melon
menu van de dag set menu
mierikswortel horseradish
milkshake milkshake
mineraalwater mineral water
met koolzuur carbonated
zonder koolzuur still
moorkop/Bossche bol puff-pastry coated in chocolate and filled with whipped cream
mossel mussel
mosterd mustard
mosterdsaus mustard sauce
mousserend sparkling

nagerecht dessert
Nasi goreng special fried rice (Indonesian)
Nasi rames a mixed rice dish, a smaller version of the **rijsttafel** (Indonesian)
net gaar gebakken medium
nier kidney
niet gaar/rood rare
nieuwe salt-cured herring
noot nut
nootmuskaat nutmeg

oester oyster
olie oil

olijf olive
omelet met champignons mushroom omelette
omelet met ham ham omelette
omelet met kaas cheese omelette
omelet naturel plain omelette
ongaar rare (not cooked)
ontbijt breakfast
ontbijtkoek spiced cake sometimes eaten at breakfast
ontbijt spek streaky bacon
oranjebitter orange-flavoured bitters
ossenhaas beef fillet
ossenstaart oxtail
ossenstaartsoep oxtail soup
ossentong beef tongue
oude jenever mature gin, aged in casks
oude kaas mature cheese

paardenbiefstuk horse meat
paddenstoel mushroom
paling eel
 paling in het groen eel stewed in white wine, served with a herb sauce
pannenkoek pancake
 pannenkoek met appel pancake with apple
 pannenkoek met spek pancake with bacon
pannenkoekenstroop pancake syrup
pannenkoekhuis pancake house
pap porridge
paprika green or red pepper

pastei pie
patat/patates frites chips
patrijs patridge
peer pear
pekeltong salted tongue
pekelvlees salted beef
peper pepper
peperkoek spiced ginger cake
perzik peach
peterselie parsley
peultjes sugar peas
piccalilly pickle
pils beer; lager
pinda peanut
pindakaas peanut butter
Pisang goreng fried banana (Indonesian)
plakken slices
poedersuiker icing sugar
poffertjes small round fritters served with icing sugar
pompelmoes grapefruit
port port
portie portion
pot jar
potje pot of
prei leek
prinsessenboon green bean
proeflokaal bar selling locally produced drinks
pruim plum

rabarber rhubarb
radijs radish
rauw raw
ravigotesaus herb sauce
reebout or **reerug** venison
reep chocolade chocolate bar
rekening bill
ribstuk rib of beef
rijst rice
rijsttafel a banquet of Indonesian dishes
rivierkreeft crayfish
rodebiet beetroot
rodekool red cabbage
Roedjak manis apple, cucumber and orange in soy sauce (Indonesian)
roerei scrambled egg
roggebrood rye bread
rolmops rollmop herring
rood red
rookspek smoked bacon
rookvlees smoked beef
rookworst smoked sausage
roomboter butter
roomijs ice-cream
rosbief roast beef
rozemarijn rosemary
rozijnen raisins
runderlap beefsteak

rundervink minced meat rolled in sliced smoked beef
rundvlees beef
Russisch ei hard-boiled eggs with potato salad

saffraan saffron
Sajoer kerrie spicy cabbage soup (Indonesian)
Sajoer lodeh vegetable, meat or shrimp soup (Indonesian)
salade salad
sambal hot pepper paste used as a condiment
sap juice
saté meat on a skewer with peanut sauce
Satej ajam chicken on a skewer with peanut sauce (Indonesian)
Sateh babi pork on a skewer with peanut sauce (Indonesian)
saucijsjes sausages
saucijzenbroodje sausage roll
saus sauce or gravy
schaal- en schelpdieren shellfish
schapenvlees mutton
schelvis haddock
selderij celery
sherry sherry
sinaasappel orange
sinas orangeade
sla lettuce
slagroom whipped cream

slak snail
slavink minced meat rolled in sliced smoked bacon
snoek pike
snoep sweets
soep soup
soep van de dag soup of the day
specerijen spices
specialiteit van het huis house speciality
speculaas spiced almond biscuit
spek bacon
sperzieboon French or green bean
spiegelei fried egg
spiegeleieren met ham fried eggs and ham
spiegeleieren met ontbijtspek fried eggs and bacon
spijskaart menu
spinazie spinach
speenvarken suckling pig
sprits shortbread
sprot sprats
spruitjes Brussels sprouts
spuitwater soda water
stamppot mashed potatoes and vegetables
sterke drank spirit
stroop treacle, syrup
stroopwafels thin, syrup-filled biscuits
studentenhaver mixed nuts and raisins
stuk piece
suiker sugar

taart cake
tarbot turbot
tartaar steak tartare
thee tea
thee met citroen lemon tea
thee met suiker en melk tea with sugar and milk
theezakje teabag
tijm thyme
Tjap tjoy chop suey (Indonesian)
toeristenmenu tourist menu
toeslag supplementary charge
tomaat tomato
tompoes iced flaky pastry slice filled with vanilla custard
tong tongue or sole
tongschar lemon sole
tonijn tuna
tonijnsalade tuna salad/tuna mayonnaise
toost toast
tosti toasted sandwich
tosti ham-kaas ham and cheese toasted sandwich
tosti hawaï ham, cheese and pineapple toasted sandwich
tournedos round fillet steak
trappistenbier heavy, usually strong beer
truffel truffle
tuinbonen broad beans

ui onion
uitsmijter slices of bread with ham, cheese or beef topped with fried egg

vanille vanilla
varkenshaas pork tenderloin
varkenskarbonade pork chop
varkensvlees pork
vegetarische vegetarian
venkel fennel
vermicellisoep consommé with noodles
vers fresh
vet fat
vieux brandy
vijg fig
vis fish
vla cold custard-like dairy product
vlaai fruit lattice tart
Vlaamse karbonade beer-braised beef
Vlaamse kool cabbage with apples and gooseberry jelly
Vlaamse hazenpeper jugged hare stew
vlees meat
vleeskroketten meat croquettes
vleeswaren cold meats
volkoren brood wholemeal bread
voorgerecht starter
vrucht fruit
vruchtensalade fruit salad

vruchtensap fruit juice
appelsap apple juice
grapefruitsap grapefruit juice
druivensap grape juice
sinaasappelsap orange juice
tomatensap tomato juice

wafel wafer or waffle
walnoot walnut
warm hot
warme chocolademelk hot chocolate
waterkers watercress
watermeloen watermelon
waterzooi meat or fish poached with vegetables and egg yolk
wegrestaurant roadside restaurant
whisky whisky
met ijs on the rocks
met water with water
wijnkaart wine list
wijting whiting
wild game
wild zwijn wild boar
wilde eend wild duck
wijn wine
droge wijn dry wine
mousserende wijn sparkling wine
huis wijn house wine
rode wijn red wine

witte wijn white wine
zoete wijn sweet wine
wijting whiting
wit white
witlof chicory
witlof op z'n Brussels baked chicory with cheese and ham
witte wijnsaus white wine sauce
wodka vodka
worst sausage
wortel carrot

yoghurt yoghurt

zachtgekookt ei soft-boiled egg
zalm salmon
zeekreeft lobster
zeetong sole
zilveruitjes pickled cocktail onions
zoet sweet
zout salt
zure haring marinated herring
zuurkool pickled cabbage
zwarte bessen blackcurrants
zwarte kersen black cherries
zwarte koffie black coffee

Grammar

Nouns and articles

Unlike English, Dutch nouns have a gender: they are either common (with the article **de**) or neuter (with the article **het**). Therefore the words for 'the' must agree with the noun they accompany – whether common, neuter or plural:

		pronunciation
the garden	**de tuin**	du tuin
the house	**het huis**	het huis
the gardens	**de tuinen**	du **tui**-nu
the houses	**de huizen**	du **hui**-zu

The word for 'a/an' is **een** with both genders:

		pronunciation
a garden	**een tuin**	un tuin
a house	**een huis**	un huis

The word **een** can have two meanings: 'a/an' or 'one', with a different pronuncation indicating the meaning:

		pronunciation
a	**een**	un
one	**een/één**	ayn

The Dutch frequently use diminutives, expressing smallness of size, endearment or contempt.
The diminutive is mostly formed by adding -**je** or -**tje**, but also -**etje**, -**pje** and -**kje**:

		pronunciation
house	**het huisje**	het **hui**-shu
garden	**het tuintje**	het **tuin**-chu
flag	**het vlaggetje**	het **vlaCH**-CHu-chu
tree	**het boompje**	het **bohm**-pyu
king	**het koninkje**	het **koh**-nink-yu

Diminutives are always neuter nouns.

Plurals

There are three ways to form the plural of nouns.

1. The most common way is by adding **-en**:

	singular	plural
tent	**tent** tent	**tenten** **ten**-tu

Note:
a. Nouns ending with a double vowel followed by a consonant drop a vowel in the plural:

	singular	plural
moon	**maan** mahn	**manen** **mah**-nu
leg	**been** bayn	**benen** **bay**-nu
school	**school** sCHohl	**scholen** **sCHoh**-lu
wall	**muur** muur	**muren** **muu**-ru

b. Many nouns ending with a single vowel followed by a consonant double that consonant in the plural:

	singular	plural
man	**man** man	**mannen** **man**-nu
bell	**bel** bel	**bellen** **bel**-lu
bone	**bot** bot	**botten** **bot**-tu

But:

	singular	plural
day	**dag** daCH	**dagen** **dah**-CHu
town	**stad** stad	**steden** **stay**-du

c. Many nouns ending with **-s** or **-f** get **-z** and **-v** in the plural:

	singular	plural
house	**huis** huis	**huizen** **hui**-zu
cousin/ nephew	**neef** nayf	**neven** **nay**-vu

But:

	singular	plural
cherry	**kers** kers	**kersen** **ker**-su

2. Nouns ending with a vowel or with -**aar**, -**el**, -**em**, -**en**, -**er**, -**erd**, -**je** form the plural with -**s**; here are some examples:

	singular	plural
table	**tafel** **tah**-fel	**tafels** **tah**-fels
car	**auto** **ow**-toh	**auto's** **ow**-tohs
umbrella	**paraplu** pah-rah-**pluu**	**paraplu's** pah-rah-**pluus**
wing	**vleugel** **vleu**-CHul	**vleugels** **vleu**-CHuls
broom	**bezem** **bay**-zem	**bezems** **bay**-zems

3. A few nouns form the plural with -**eren**:

	singular	plural
child	**kind** kint	**kinderen** **kin**-du-ru

This, that, these, those...

Demonstratives depend on the gender of the noun:

	this	that	these	those
de tuin	**deze tuin**	**die tuin**	**deze tuinen**	**die tuinen**
het huis	**dit huis**	**dat huis**	**deze huizen**	**die huizen**

Note: pronunciation **deze** **day**-zu

Adjectives

The adjective is placed before the noun as follows:

small	**klein**	klein
	de kleine tuin	de **klein**-u tuin
	een kleine tuin	un **klein**-u tuin
	het kleine huis	het **klein**-u huis
	een klein huis	un **klein** huis

Pronouns

subject		object		possessive	
I	**ik**	me	**me**	my	**mijn**
you	**jij/je**	you	**je**	your	**jouw**
you (singular and plural: formal)	**u**	you	**u**	your	**uw**
he	**hij**	him	**hem**	his	**zijn**
she	**zij/ze**	her	**haar**	her	**haar**
it	**het**	it	**het**	its	**–**
we	**wij/we**	us	**ons**	our	**onze/ons**
you	**jullie**	you	**jullie**	your	**jullie**
they	**zij/ze**	them	**hen**	their	**hun**

Note: **de tuin** **onze tuin**
het huis **ons huis**

Questions

who/whom **wie**
what **wat**
why **waarom**
which **welke/welk**

Note: **de tuin** **welke tuin**
het huis **welk huis**

Verbs

Some useful verbs:

zijn to be

	present	past
I	**ben**	**was**
you	**bent**	**was**
he/she/it	**is**	**was**
we	**zijn**	**waren**
you	**zijn**	**waren**
they	**zijn**	**waren**

hebben to have

	present	past
I	**heb**	**had**
you	**hebt**	**had**
he/she/it	**heeft**	**had**
we	**hebben**	**hadden**
you	**hebben**	**hadden**
they	**hebben**	**hadden**

mogen to be allowed

	present	past
I	**mag**	**mocht**
you	**mag**	**mocht**
he/she/it	**mag**	**mocht**
we	**mogen**	**mochten**
you	**mogen**	**mochten**
they	**mogen**	**mochten**

moeten to have to

	present	past
I	**moet**	**moest**
you	**moet**	**moest**
he/she/it	**moet**	**moest**
we	**moeten**	**moesten**
you	**moeten**	**moesten**
they	**moeten**	**moesten**

willen to want to

	present	past
I	**wil**	**wou, wilde**
you	**wilt**	**wou, wilde**
he/she/it	**wil**	**wou, wilde**
we	**willen**	**wilden**
you	**willen**	**wilden**
they	**willen**	**wilden**

Note: When **jij** follows the verb, the end **-t** of the verb is lost:

you have	**jij hebt**
have you?	**heb jij?**
you want	**jij wilt**
do you want?	**wil jij?**

The English continuous form is unknown in Dutch:

I am going away	**ik ga weg**
I am going home	**ik ga naar huis**

Equally, questions and negatives use the simple verb form:

are you going home?	**ga jij naar huis?**
do you go home?	**ga jij naar huis?**
don't go!	**ga niet!**

Public holidays

Fixed

January 1	**Nieuwjaarsdag** New Year's Day
April 30	**Koninginnedag** Queen's official birthday
May 4*	**Dodenherdenking** Remembrance Day
May 5°	**Bevrijdingsdag** Liberation Day
December 5*	**Pakjesavond/Sinterklaas** Eve of Saint Nicholas
December 25	**Eerste Kerstdag** Christmas Day
December 26	**Tweede Kerstdag** Boxing Day
December 31*	**Nieuwjaarsavond/Oud & Nieuw** New Year's Eve

* not an official public holiday

° celebrated every year but, as of 2000, an official holiday only once every 5 years

Movable

Friday before Easter	**Goede Vrijdag** Good Friday
Easter	**Eerste Paasdag** Easter Sunday
Monday after Easter	**Tweede Paasdag** Easter Monday
6th Thursday after Easter	**Hemelvaart** Ascension
7th Sunday after Easter	**Pinksteren** Pentecost/ Whit Sunday
7th Monday after Easter	**Tweede Pinksterdag** Whit Monday

English - Dutch

A

English	Dutch	Pronunciation
a (an)	een	un
able: ***to be able (to)***	kunnen	**kuen**-nu
about (roughly)	ongeveer	**on**-CHu-vayr
a book about...	een boek over...	un book **oh**-ver...
about ten o'clock	ongeveer tien uur	**on**-CHu-vayr **teen** uur
above	boven	**boh**-vu
abroad	buitenland	**bui**-tun-lant
to go abroad	naar het buitenland gaan	nahr ut **bui**-ten-lant CHahn
access	toegang, de	**too**-CHang
accessible for wheelchair access	toegankelijk voor rolstoelen	too-**CHang**-ke-luk vohr **rol**-stool-lu
accident	ongeluk, het	**on**-CHu-luk
accident & emergency department	EHBO	ay-ha-bay-oh
accommodation	accommodatie, de	ac-com-moh-**dah**-tsee
account	rekening, de	**ray**-ku-ning
to ache	pijn doen	pein doon
my head aches	mijn hoofd doet pijn	mein hohft doot pein
address	adres, het	ah-**dres**
admission charge/fee	toegangsgeld, het; entree, de	**too**-CHangs-CHelt; on-**tray**
adult	volwassene, de	vol-**was**-su-nu
for adults	voor volwassenen	vohr vol-**was**-su-nu
to advise	adviseren	ad-vee-**sayr**-ru
A&E	EHBO	ay-ha-bay-oh
aeroplane	vliegtuig, het	**vleeCH**-tuiCH
afraid: ***to be afraid of***	bang zijn voor	bang zein vohr
after	na	nah
after lunch	na de lunch	nah du lunch
afternoon	middag, de	**mid**-daCH

this afternoon	vanmiddag	van-**mid**-daCH
in the afternoon	's middags	**smid**-daCH-s
tomorrow afternoon	morgenmiddag	mor-CHu-**mid**-daCH
again	weer	wayr
against	tegen	**tay**-CHu
age	leeftijd, de	**layf**-teit
ago: 2 *days ago*	twee dagen geleden	tway **dah**-CHu CHu-**lay**-du
agreement	overeenkomst, de	oh-ver-**ayn**-komst
air conditioning	air conditioning, de	**air**-con-di-si-syoh-ning
airplane	vliegtuig, het	**vleeCH**-tuiCH
airport	vliegveld, het	**vleeCH**-velt
airport bus	vliegveldbus, de	**vleeCH**-velt-bues
air ticket	tickets, de	**tick**-ets
alarm	alarm, het	ah-**larm**
alarm clock	wekker, de	**wek**-ker
alcohol	alcohol, de	**al**-coh-hol
alcohol-free	alcoholvrij	al-coh-hol-**vrei**
alcoholic	alcoholische	al-coh-**hohl**-ee-su
all	alle	**al**-lu
allergic	allergisch	al-**ler**-CHees
I'm allergic to	ik ben allergisch voor	ik ben al-**ler**-CHees vohr
allergy	allergie, de	al-ler-**CHee**
to allow	toestaan	**too**-stahn
all right	OK	oh-**kay**
are you all right?	ben je OK?	ben yu oh-**kay**?
almost	bijna	**bei**-nah
alone	alleen	al-**layn**
already	al	al
also	ook	ohk
always	altijd	al-**teit**
a.m.	voor de middag	vohr du **mid**-daCH
ambulance	ambulance, de	am-buu-**lan**-su
America	Amerika	a-**may**-ree-kah

American Amerikaans a-may-ree-**kahns**
anaesthetic verdoving, de ver-**doh**-ving
and en en
angry boos bohs
annual jaarlijks **yahr**-luks
another (one) nog een noCH ayn
another beer? nog een bier? noCH ayn beer?
answer antwoord, het **ant**-wohrt
to answer antwoorden **ant**-wohr-du
answerphone antwoordapparaat, het **ant**-wohrd-ap-pah-**raht**
antacid maagzuur neutraliserend **mahCH**-zuur neu-trah-lee-**sayr**-runt
antibiotics antibiotica, de an-tee-bee-**oh**-tee-cah
antihistamine antihistaminicum an-tee-his-tah-**mee**-nee-cuem
antiseptic ontsmettend middel, de ont-**smet**-unt **mid**-del

any (some) enige **ay**-ni-CHu
(negative) geen CHayn
I haven't any money ik heb geen geld ik heb CHayn CHelt
anyone (in questions) iemand **ee**-munt
anything (in questions) iets eets
anywhere ergens **er**-CHuns
(negative) nergens **ner**-CHuns
apple appel, de **ap**-pul
approximately ongeveer **on**-Chu-vayr
apricot abrikoos, de ab-ree-**kohs**
arm arm, de arm
to arrange regelen **ray**-CHu-lu
to arrest arresteren ar-rest-**ayr**-ru
arrival aankomst, de **ahn**-komst
to arrive aankomen **ahn**-koh-mu
art kunst kuenst
ashtray asbak, de **as**-bak
to ask vragen **vrah**-CHu

English	Dutch	Pronunciation
asparagus	asperge, de	as-**per**-shu
aspirin	aspirine, de	as-pee-**ree**-nu
asthma	astma, de	**ast**-mah
I have asthma	ik heb astma	ik heb **ast**-mah
at	in; bij; om	in; bei; om
at home	thuis	tuis
at 8 o'clock	om acht uur	om aCHt uur
at once	direct	dee-**rect**
ATM	geldautomaat, de	**CHelt**-ow-toh-maht
attractive (person)	aantrekkelijk	ahn-**trek**-ku-luk
August	augustus	ow-**CHues**-tues
Australia	Australië	ow-**strah**-lee-u
Australian	Australisch	ow-**strah**-lees
automatic	automatisch	ow-toh-**mah**-tees
autumn	herfst, de	herfst
available	beschikbaar	bu-**sCHik**-bahr
to avoid	ontwijken	ont-**wei**-ku
awake	wakker	**wak**-ker
awful	verschrikkelijk	ver-**sCHrik**-ku-luk

B

English	Dutch	Pronunciation
baby	baby, de	**ba**by
baby food	babyvoeding, de	**ba**by-vood-ing
baby milk	babymelk, de	**ba**by-melk
baby seat (in car)	kinderzitje, het	**kin**-der-zit-chu
baby-sitter	oppasser, de	**op**-pas-ser
back (of body)	rug, de	rueCH
back (to go/ give back)	terug	tu-**rueCH**
bad (weather, news)	slecht	sleCHt
(fruit, vegetables)	bedorven	bu-**dor**-vu
bag	tas, de	tas
(handbag)	handtas, de	**hant**-tas
(case)	koffer, de	**kof**-fer
baggage	bagage, de	bah-**CHah**-shu
baked	gebakken	CHu-**bak**-ku

English – Dutch

baker	bakker, de	**bak**-ker
banana	banaan, de	bah-**nahn**
bank	bank, de	bank
bank account	bankrekening, de	bank-**ray**-ku-ning
banknote	bankbiljet, het	**bank**-bil-yet
bar	bar, de; café, het	bar; ca-**fay**
bath	bad, het	bat
to have a bath	een bad nemen	un bat **nay**-mu
bathroom	badkamer, de	**bat**-kah-mer
with bathroom	met badkamer	met **bat**-kah-mer
battery	batterij, de	bat-ter-**rei**
(for car)	accu, de	**ak**-kuu
B&B	pension, het	pen-**shon**
to be	zijn	zein
beach	strand, het	strant
bean	boon, de	bohn
beautiful	mooi	**moh**-ee
because	omdat	**om**-dat
to become	worden	**wor**-du
bed	bed, het	bet
double bed	tweepersoons-bed, het	**tway**-per-sohns-bet
single bed	eenpersoonsbed, het	**ayn**-per-sohns-bet
bedroom	slaapkamer, de	**slahp**-kah-mer
beef	rundvlees, het	**ruent**-vlays
beer	bier, het	beer
before	voor	vohr
before breakfast	voor het ontbijt	vohr ut ont-**beit**
to begin	beginnen	bu-**CHin**-nu
behind	achter	**aCH**-ter
Belgian	Belgisch	**bel**-CHees
(person)	Belg	belCH
Belgium	België	**bel**-CHee-yu
to believe	geloven	CHu-**loh**-vu
below	onder	**on**-der
(less than)	minder dan	**min**-der dan
beside (next to)	naast	nahst
best: *the best*	de beste	du **best**-u
better (than)	beter (dan)	**bay**-ter (dan)

between	tussen	**tues**-su
bicycle	fiets, de	feets
by bicycle	met de fiets	met du feets
big	groot	CHroht
bigger (than)	groter dan	**CHroh**-ter dan
bill (for payment)	rekening, de	**ray**-ku-ning
birthday	verjaardag, de	ver-**yahr**-daCH
happy birthday	hartelijk gefeliciteerd met je verjaardag	**har**-tu-luk CHu-**fay**-lee-see-tayrt met yu ver-**yahr**-daCH
my birthday is on...	ik ben jarig op...	ik ben **yah**-riCH op...
birthday card	verjaardagskaart, de	ver-**yahr**-daCHs-kahrt
biscuits	koekjes, de	**kook**-yus
bit: ***a bit***	een beetje	un **bay**-chu
bite (of animal, insect)	beet, de	bayt
let's have a bite to eat	laten we wat eten	**lah**-tu wu wat **ay**-tu
bitten (by animal, insect)	gebeten	CHu-**bay**-tu
black	zwart	zwart
to bleed	bloeden	**bloo**-du
blister	blaar, de	blahr
block of flats	flatgebouw, het	**flet**-CHu-bow
blood	bloed, het	bloot
blood pressure	bloeddruk, de	**bloot**-drook
blood test	bloedtest, de	**bloot**-test
to blow-dry	föhnen	**feu**-nu
blue	blauw	blow
boarding house	pension, het	pen-**shon**
body	lichaam, het	**liCH**-ahm
to boil	koken	**koh**-ku
boiled	gekookt	CHu-**kohkt**
book	boek, het	book
to book	reserveren	ray-ser-**vayr**-ru
booking	reservering, de	ray-ser-**vayr**-ring
boots	laarzen, de	**lahr**-zu
border	grens, de	CHrens

English	Dutch	Pronunciation
boring	saai	**sah**-ee
boss	baas, de; chef, de	bahs; shef
both	allebei	al-lu-**bei**
bottle	fles, de	fles
a bottle of wine	een fles wijn	un fles wein
bottle opener	flesopener, de	**fles**-oh-pun-er
box	doos, de	dohs
box office	reserveringen; kassa, de	ray-ser-**vay**-ring-u; **kas**-sa
boy	jongen, de	**yong**-u
boyfriend	vriend, de	vreent
bra	beha, de	bay-**hah**
to brake	remmen	**rem**-mu
brakes	remmen, de	**rem**-mu
brand (make)	merk, het	merk
bread	brood, het	broht
wholemeal bread	volkorenbrood, het	vol-**koh**-ru-broht
bread roll	broodje, het	**broht**-chu
to break	breken	**bray**-ku
breakdown (car)	autopech, de	**ow**-toh-peCH
breakfast	ontbijt, het	ont-**beit**
breast	borst, de	borst
to breathe	ademen	**ah**-du-mu
briefcase	aktentas, de	**ak**-tu-tas
to bring	brengen	**breng**-u
Britain	Groot Brittannië	CHroht brit-**tan**-nee-yu
British	Brits	brits
broad	breed	brayt
brochure	brochure, de	broh-**shuu**-ru
broken	gebroken	CHu-**broh**-ku
broken down (car, etc)	kapot	kah-**pot**
brother	broer, de	broor
brown	bruin	bruin
bruise	blauwe plek, de	**blow**-wu plek
building	gebouw, het	CHu-**bow**

English	Dutch	Pronunciation
bulb (flower)	bloembol, de	**bloom**-bol
bunch (of flowers)	boeket, het	boo-**ket**
bureau de change	wisselkantoor, het	**wis**-sul-kan-tohr
burger	hamburger, de	**ham**-buer-CHer
burglary	inbraak, de	**in**-brahk
bus	bus, de	bues
bus stop	bushalte, de	**bues**-hal-tu
bus ticket (multiple)	strippenkaart, de	**strip**-pu-kahrt
business	zaken	**zah**-ku
on business	voor zaken	vohr **zah**-ku
business trip	zakenreis, de	**zah**-kun-reis
busy	druk	druek
but	maar	mahr
butcher	slager, de	**slah**-CHer
butter	boter, de	**boh**-ter
to buy	kopen	**koh**-pu
by	door; met	dohr; met;
(near)	bij	bei
(next to)	naast	nahst
by bus	met de bus	met du bues
by car	met de auto	met du **ow**-toh
by train	met de trein	met du trein

C

English	Dutch	Pronunciation
cab (taxi)	taxi, de	**tak**-see
café	café, het	ca-**fay**
internet café	internet café, het	**in**ternet ca-**fay**
cake	taart, de; gebak, het	tahrt; CHu-**bak**
cake shop	banketbakker, de	bang-**ket**-bak-ker
to call	roepen	**roo**-pu
(to phone)	bellen	**bel**-lu
call (telephone)	gesprek, het	CHu-**sprek**
calm	kalm	kalm
camera	camera, de	**kah**-mu-rah
to camp	kamperen	kam-**payr**-ru

English	Dutch	Pronunciation
campsite	camping, de	**kem**-ping
can (to be able)	kunnen	**kuen**-nu
I can	ik kan	ik kan
we can	we kunnen	wu **kuen**-nu
I cannot	ik kan niet	ik kan neet
we cannot	we kunnen niet	wu **kuen**-nu neet
can I...?	kan ik...?	kan ik...?
can we...?	kunnen we?	**kuen**-nu wu?
can	blikje, het	**blik**-yu
can opener	blikopener, de	**blik**-oh-pun-er
Canadian	Canadees	cah-nah-**days**
to cancel	annuleren	an-nuu-**layr**-ru
cancellation	annulering, de	an-nuu-**lay**-ring
capital (city)	hoofdstad, de	**hohft**-stat
car	auto, de	**ow**-toh
car ferry	autoveerboot, de	**ow**-toh-vayr-boht
car hire	autoverhuur, de	**ow**-toh-ver-**huur**
car insurance	autoverzekering, de	**ow**-toh-ver-**zay**-ker-ing
car keys	autosleutels, de	**ow**-toh-**sleu**-tels
car park	parkeerplaats, de	par-**kayr**-plahts
careful	voorzichtig	vohr-**ziCH**-tiCH
be careful!	wees voorzichtig!	ways vohr-**ziCH**-tiCH!
carriage	wagon, de	wa-**CHon**
carrot	wortel, de	**wor**-tel
to carry	dragen	**drah**-CHu
case (suitcase)	koffer, de	**kof**-fer
cash	contant	con-**tant**
to cash (cheque)	inwisselen	**in**-wis-su-lu
cash desk	kassa, de	**kas**-sah
cash dispenser	geldautomaat, de	**CHelt**-ow-toh-maht
castle	slot, het	slot
casualty department	EHBO, de; ongevallen-afdeling, de	ay-hah-bay-oh; **on**-CHu-val-lu-**af**-day-ling
cat	kat, de	kat
to catch (bus, train, etc)	nemen	**nay**-mu

English	Dutch	Pronunciation
cathedral	kathedraal, de	ka-tu-**drahl**
Catholic	katholiek	ka-toh-**leek**
caulifower	bloemkool, de	**bloom**-kohl
cave	grot, de	CHrot
CD player	CD speler, de	say-**day spay**-ler
cellphone	mobiele telefoon, de; gsm, de	moh-**bee**-lu **tay**-lu-fohn; **CHay**-es-em
cent	cent, de	sent
central	centraal	sen-**trahl**
centre	centrum, het	**sen**-truem
century	eeuw, de	**ay**-oo
cereal (for breakfast)	cornflakes, de	cornflakes
certain	zeker	**zay**-ker
chain	ketting, de	**ket**-ting
chair	stoel, de	stool
change (coins)	kleingeld, het	**klein**-CHelt
(money returned)	wisselgeld, het	**wis**-sul-CHelt
to change	veranderen	ver-**an**-du-ru
to change money	wisselen	**wis**-su-lu
to change clothes	verkleden	ver-**klay**-du
to change trains	overstappen	**oh**-ver-stap-u
Channel: *the English Channel*	Kanaal, het	kah-**nahl**
to charge (fee)	rekenen	**ray**-ku-nu
please charge it to my account	zet het op mijn rekening, alstublieft	zet ut op mein **ray**-ku-ning, als-tuu-**bleeft**
to charge (phone)	opladen	**op**-lah-du
I need to charge my phone	ik moet mijn telefoon opladen	ik moot mein **tay**-lu-fohn **op**-lah-du
charger (for battery)	oplader, de	**op**-lah-der
cheap	goedkoop	CHoot-**kohp**
cheaper	goedkoper	CHoot-**koh**-per

English	Dutch	Pronunciation
to check	controleren	con-troh-**layr**-ru
to check in (at airport)	inchecken	**in**-check-u
(at hotel)	inschrijven	**in**-sCHrei-vu
cheers	proost	prohst
cheese	kaas, de	kahs
chemist	drogist, de; apotheek, de	droh-**CHist**; ah-poh-**tayk**
cheque	cheque, de	check
chequebook	chequeboek, het	**check**-book
cheque card	betaalpas, de	bu-**tahl**-pas
cherries	kersen, de	**ker**-su
chest (of body)	borst, de	borst
chicken	kip, de	kip
chicken breast	kipfilet, de	kip-fee-**lay**
child	kind, het	kint
children	kinderen, de	**kin**-du-ru
chips	patat (patates frites), de	pa-**tat** (pa-**tat** freet)
chocolate	chocolade, de	shoh-koh-**lah**-du
chocolates	bonbons, de	bon-**bons**
choice	keuze, de	**keu**-zu
to choose	kiezen	**kee**-zu
Christmas	Kerstmis	**kerst**-mis
merry Christmas!	Vrolijk Kerstfeest!	**vroh**-luk **kerst**-fayst!
church	kerk, de	kerk
cigarette	sigaret, de	see-CHah-**ret**
cigarette lighter	aansteker, de	**ahn**-stay-ker
cigarette papers	vloeitjes, de	**vloo**-ee-chus
cinema	bioscoop, de	bee-oh-**skohp**
city	stad, de	stat
city centre	centrum, het	**sen**-truem
class: ***first class***	eerste klas	**ayr**-stu klas
second class	tweede klas	**tway**-du klas
clean	schoon	sCHohn
to clean	schoonmaken	**sCHohn**-mah-ku
client	klant, de	klant

English	Dutch	Pronunciation
to climb	klimmen	**klim**-mu
clinic	kliniek, de	klee-**neek**
clock	klok, de	klok
clogs	klompen, de	**klom**-pu
to close	sluiten	**slui**-tu
closed	gesloten	CHu-**sloh**-tu
clothes	kleren, de	**klayr**-ru
cloudy	bewolkt	bu-**wolkt**
coach	bus, de	bues
coast	kust, de	kuest
coat	jas, de	yas
coconut	kokosnoot, de	**koh**-kos-noht
cod	kabeljauw, de	kah-bel-**yow**
coffee	koffie, de	**kof**-fee
white coffee	koffie met melk	**kof**-fee met melk
decaffeinated coffee	cafeïnevrije koffie	caf-ay-**ee**-nu-vrei-u **kof**-fee
coin	munt, de	muent
Coke™	Cola, de	**coh**-lah
cold	koud	kowt
I'm cold	ik heb het koud	ik heb ut kowt
it's cold	het is koud	ut is kowt
cold water	koud water	kowt **wah**-ter
cold (illness)	verkoudheid, de	ver-**kowt**-heit
I have a cold	ik ben verkouden	ik ben ver-**kow**-du
cold sore	koortsuitslag, de	**kohrts**-uit-slaCH
colleague	collega, de	col-**lay**-CHah
to collect	ophalen	**op**-hah-lu
colour	kleur, de	kleur
to come	komen	**koh**-mu
(arrive)	aankomen	**ahn**-koh-mu
to come back	terugkomen	tu-**rueCH**-koh-mu
to come in	binnenkomen	**bin**-nu-koh-mu
come in!	kom binnen!	kom **bin**-nu
comfortable	comfortabel	com-for-**tah**-bel
company (firm)	bedrijf, het	bu-**dreif**
compartment (in train)	coupé, de	coo-**pay**
to complain	klagen	**klah**-CHu
complaint	klacht, de	klaCHt

English	Dutch	Pronunciation
complete	compleet	com-**playt**
to complete	compleet maken	com-**playt** **mah**-ku
computer	computer, de	com-**puu**-ter
concert	concert, het	con-**sert**
concession	korting, de	**kor**-ting
conditioner	crèmespoeling, de	**crehm**-spoo-ling
condom	condoom, het	kon-**dohm**
cone (ice cream)	hoorntje, het	**hohrn**-chu
conference	conferentie, de	con-fu-**ren**-see
to confirm	bevestigen	bu-**ves**-tiCH-u
confirmation (of booking)	bevestiging, de	bu-**ves**-tiCH-ing
confused	in de war	in du war
congratulations!	gefeliciteerd!	CHu-**fay**-lee-see-**tayrt**!
connection (flight, etc)	verbinding, de	ver-**bin**-ding
consulate	consulaat, het	con-soo-**laht**
to contact	contact opnemen met	con-**tact op**-neh-mu met
contact lenses	contactlenzen, de	con-**tact**-len-zu
to continue	doorgaan	**dohr**-CHahn
contraceptive	voorbehoedsmiddel, het	**vohr**-bu-hoods-**mid**-del
emergency contraception	noodvoorbehoedsmiddel, het	**noht**-vohr-bu-hoods-**mid**-del
to cook	koken	**koh**-ku
cooked	gekookt	CHu-**kohkt**
cooker	fornuis, het	for-**nuis**
cookies	koekjes, de	**cook**-yus
cool	koel	cool
copy	kopie, de	koh-**pee**
corkscrew	kurkentrekker, de	**kuer**-ku-trek-ker
corner	hoek, de	hook
corridor	gang, de	CHang
to cost	kosten	**kos**-tu
how much does it cost?	hoeveel kost het?	**hoo**-vayl kost ut?

English	Dutch	Pronunciation
costume, (swimming) (men)	zwembroek, de	**zwem**-brook
(women)	zwempak, het	**zwem**-pak
cotton wool	watten, de	**wat**-tu
to cough	hoesten	**hoos**-tu
cough	hoest, de	hoost
counter (shop, bar etc)	toonbank, de	**tohn**-bank
country	land, het	lant
countryside	platteland, het	**plat**-u-lant
couple (two people)	paar, het	pahr
a couple of...	een paar...	un pahr...
(a few)	enkele	**eng**-ku-lu
course (of meal)	gang, de	CHang
(of study)	cursus, de	**kuer**-sues
cousin	neef, de	nayf
cover charge	couverttoeslag, de	coo-**vair**-too-slaCH
crafts	ambachten, de	**am**-baCH-tu
crash (car)	aanrijding, de	**ahn**-rei-ding
to crash	verongelukken	ver-**on**-CHu-luek-ku
cream (lotion)	crème, de	crehm
(dairy)	room, de	rohm
whipped cream	slagroom, de	**slaCH**-rohm
credit (on mobile phone)	beltegoed, het	**bel**-tu-CHoot
credit card	credit card, de	**cre**-dit-card
crime	misdaad, de	**mis**-daht
crisps	chips, de	ships
to cross (road)	oversteken	**oh**-ver-stay-ku
crossroads	kruispunt, het	**kruis**-puent
crowd	menigte, de	**may**-niCH-tu
crowded	druk	druek
to cry (weep)	huilen	**hui**-lu
cucumber	komkommer, de	kom-**kom**-mer
cup	kop, de	kop
currency	valuta, de	vah-**luu**-tah
customer	klant, de	klant

customs (at airport etc)	douane, de	doo-**ah**-nu
to cut	snijden	**snei**-du
to cycle	fietsen	**feet**-su
cycle path	fietspad, het	**feets**-pat
cystitis	blaasontsteking, de	**blahs**-ont-stay-king

D

daily	dagelijks	**dah**-CHu-luks
dairy produce	zuivelprodukten, de	**zui**-vul-proh-duek-tu
damage	schade, de	**sCHah**-du
damp	vochtig	**voCH**-tiCH
to dance	dansen	**dan**-su
danger	gevaar, het	CHu-**vahr**
dangerous	gevaarlijk	CHu-**vahr**-luk
dark	donker	**dong**-ker
after dark	na zonsondergang	nah zons-**on**-der-CHang
date	datum, de	**dah**-tuem
date of birth	geboortedatum, de	CHu-**bohr**-tu-**dah**-tuem
daughter	dochter, de	**doCH**-ter
day	dag, de	daCH
every day	iedere dag	**ee**-du-ru daCH
per day	per dag	per daCH
dead	dood	doht
deaf	doof	dohf
dear (on letter)	beste	**bes**-tu
(expensive)	duur	duur
debt	schuld, de	sCHuelt
debit card	debietkaart, de; pinpas, de	deb-**eet** kahrt; **pin**-pas
decaffeinated coffee	cafeïnevrije koffie, de	ca-fay-**ee**-nu-vrei-u **kof**-fee
do you have decaffeinated?	Heeft u cafeïnevrij?	hayft uu ca-fay-**ee**-nu-vrei?
to declare:		
nothing to declare	niets aan te geven	neets ahn tu **CHay**-vu

deep	diep	deep
delay	vertraging, de	ver-**trah**-CHing
how long is the delay?	hoeveel vertraging is er?	**hoo**-vayl ver-**trah**-CHing is er?
delayed	vertraagd	ver-**trahCHt**
delicious	heerlijk	**hehr**-luk
dentist	tandarts, de	**tant**-arts
deodorant	deodorant, de	day-oh-doh-**rant**
to depart	vertrekken	ver-**trek**-u
department store	warenhuis, het	**wah**-ru-huis
departure	vertrek, het	ver-**trek**
departure lounge	vertrekhal, de	ver-**trek**-hal
to describe	beschrijven	bu-**sCHrei**-vu
description	beschrijving, de	bu-**sCHrei**-ving
desk	bureau, het	buu-**roh**
(in hotel)	receptie, de	ru-**sep**-sie
dessert	dessert, het	du-**sair**
details	details, de	day-**tice**
to develop	ontwikkelen	ont-**wik**-ku-lu
diabetic (food)	voor diabetici	vohr dee-ah-**bay**-tee-see
I'm diabetic	ik heb diabetes; ik heb suikerziekte	ik heb dee-ah-**bay**-tis; ik heb **sui**-ker-zeek-te
to dial	draaien	**drah**-ee-yu
dialling code	netnummer, het	**net**-nuem-mer
dialling tone	kiestoon, de	**kees**-tohn
diaper	luier, de	**lui**-yer
dictionary	woordenboek, het	**wohr**-du-book
to die	sterven	**ster**-vu
diet	dieet, het	dee-**ayt**
I'm on a diet	ik ben op dieet	ik ben op dee-**ayt**
different	anders	**an**-ders
difficult	moeilijk	**moo**-ee-luk
digital camera	digitale camera, de	dee-CHee-**tah**-lu **kah**-mu-rah
dining room	eetkamer, de	**ayt**-kah-mer

English	Dutch	Pronunciation
dinner	diner, het	dee-**nay**
to have dinner	dineren	dee-**nayr**-ru
direct	direct	dee-**rect**
directions:		
to ask for directions	de weg vragen	de weCH **vrah**-CHu
directory (phone)	telefoonboek, het	**tay**-lu-fohn-book
dirty	vuil	vuil
disabled	gehandicapt; invalide	CHu-**han**-dee-capt; in-vah-**lee**-du
disabled person	invalide, de	in-vah-**lee**-du
to disagree	het niet eens zijn	ut neet ayns zein
disaster	ramp, de	ramp
discount	korting, de	**kor**-ting
to discover	ontdekken	ont-**dek**-u
disease	ziekte, de	**zeek**-tu
disk (computer)	schijf, de	sCHeif
floppy disk	diskette, de	dis-**ket**-u
hard disk	harde schijf, de	**har**-du sCHeif
disposable	wegwerp	**weCH**-werp
distance	afstand, de	**af**-stant
district	district, het	dis-**trict**
to disturb	storen	**stoh**-ru
diversion	afleiding, de	**af**-lei-ding
(road)	omleiding, de	**om**-lei-ding
divorced	gescheiden	CHu-**sCHei**-du
I'm divorced	ik ben gescheiden	ik ben CHu-**sCHei**-du
dizzy	duizelig	**dow**-zu-liCH
to do	doen	doon
doctor	dokter, de; arts, de	**dok**-ter; arts
documents	documenten, de	doh-cuu-**men**-tu
dog	hond, de	hont
dollar	dollar, de	**dol**-lar
domestic flight	binnenlandse vlucht, de	**bin**-nu-lant-se vlueCHt
donor card	donorcodicil, het	**doh**-nor-coh-dee-seel

English	Dutch	Pronunciation
door	deur, de	deur
double	dubbel	**dueb**-bel
double bed	tweepersoons-bed, het	**tway**-per-sohns-bet
double room	tweepersoons-kamer, de	**tway**-per-sohns-**kah**-mer
down:		
to go down	naar beneden gaan	nahr bu-**nay**-du CHahn
downstairs	beneden	bu-**nay**-du
draught (of air)	tocht, de	toCHt
there's a draught	het tocht	ut toCHt
draught lager	tapbier, het	**tap**-beer
dress	jurk, de	yuerk
to dress (oneself)	zich aankleden	ziCH **ahn**-klay-du
dressing (for salad)	slasaus, de	**slah**-sows
(for wound)	verband, het	ver-**bant**
drink	drank, de	drank
to drink	drinken	**dring**-ku
drinking water	drinkwater, het	**drink**-wah-ter
to drive	rijden	**rei**-du
driver	chauffeur, de	shoh-**feur**
driving licence	rijbewijs, het	**rei**-bu-weis
to drown	verdrinken	ver-**dring**-ku
drug (medicine)	medicijn, het	may-dee-**sein**
(narcotic)	drug, de	drueCH
drunk	dronken	**drong**-ku
dry	droog	drohCH
to dry	drogen	**droh**-CHu
dry-cleaner	stomerij, de	stoh-mu-**rei**
during	gedurende	CHu-**duur**-run-du
Dutch	Nederlands	**nay**-der-lants
Dutchman/woman	Nederlander/Nederlandse	**nay**-der-lan-der/**nay**-der-lant-su
duty-free	belastingvrij	bu-**las**-ting-vrei
DVD-player	DVD-speler, de	day-vay-day-**spay**-ler

E

English	Dutch	Pronunciation
each	elk(e); ieder(e)	**elk**-u; **ee**-du-ru
ear	oor, het	ohr
earache	oorpijn, de	**ohr**-pein
I have earache	ik heb oorpijn	ik heb **ohr**-pein
earlier	vroeger	**vroo**-CHer
early	vroeg	vrooCH
earphones	koptelefoon, de	**kop**-tay-lu-fohn
east	oost	ohst
Easter	Pasen	**pah**-su
Happy Easter!	Vrolijk Pasen!	**vroh**-luk **pah**-su!
easy	gemakkelijk	CHu-**mak**-u-luk
to eat	eten	**ay**-tu
eel	paling, de	**pah**-ling
egg	ei, het	ei
eggs	eieren, de	**ei**-yu-ru
fried egg	gebakken ei, het	CHu-**bak**-ku ei
hard-boiled egg	hard gekookt ei, het	hart CHu-**kohkt** ei
scrambled eggs	roereieren, de	**ruur**-ei-yu-ru
soft-boiled egg	zacht gekookt ei, het	zaCHt CHu-**kohkt** ei
either... or...	of... of...	of... of...
elastoplast	pleister, de	**play**-ster
electric	elektrisch	ay-**lek**-trees
electricity	elektriciteit, de	ay-lek-tree-see-**teit**
e-mail	e-mail, de	**ee**-mayl
to e-mail someone	iemand een e-mail sturen	**ee**-mant un **ee**-mayl **stuur**-ru
e-mail address	e-mail adres, het	**ee**-mayl ah-**dres**
embassy	ambassade, de	am-bah-**sah**-du
emergency	noodgeval, het	**noht**-CHu-val
emergency exit	nooduitgang, de	**noht**-owt-CHang
empty	leeg	layCH
end	einde, het	**ein**-du

engaged (to be married)	verloofd	ver-**lohft**
(phone, toilet, etc)	bezet	bu-**zet**
England	Engeland	**eng**-u-lant
English	Engels	**eng**-els
to enjoy oneself	genieten	CHu-**nee**-tu
I enjoy swimming	ik hou van zwemmen	ik how van **zwem**-mu
I enjoy dancing	ik hou van dansen	ik how van **dan**-su
enjoy your meal!	smakelijk eten!	**smah**-ku-luk **ay**-tu!
enough	genoeg	CHu-**nooCH**
that's enough	dat is genoeg	dat is CHu-**nooCH**
enquiries	inlichtingen, de	**in**-liCH-ting-u
to enter	binnenkomen	**bin**-u-koh-mu
entrance	ingang, de	**in**-CHang
entrance fee	toegangsgeld, het	**too**-CHangs-CHelt
equal (to)	gelijk (aan)	CHu-**leik** (ahn)
epileptic	epilepticus, de	ay-pee-**lep**-tee-cues
error	fout, de	fowt
to escape	ontsnappen	ont-**snap**-u
essential	essentieel	es-sen-see-**ayl**
euro	euro	eu-**roh**
Europe	Europa	eu-**roh**-pah
European	Europees	eu-roh-**pays**
evening	avond, de	**ah**-vont
in the evening	's avonds	**sah**-vonts
this evening	vanavond	van-**ah**-vont
tomorrow evening	morgenavond	mor-CHun-**ah**-vont
every	ieder	**ee**-der
everyone	iedereen	ee-der-**ayn**
everything	alles	**al**-les
everywhere	overal	**oh**-ver-al
example:		
for example	bijvoorbeeld	bei-**vohr**-baylt
excellent	uitstekend	uit-**stay**-kunt

English	Dutch	Pronunciation
except	behalve	bu-**hal**-vu
to exchange	wisselen	**wis**-su-lu
exchange rate	wisselkoers, de	**wis**-sel-koors
exciting	opwindend	**op**-win-dunt
to excuse	excuseren	ex-cuu-**sayr**-ru
excuse me!	pardon!	par-**don**!
exercise (physical)	oefening, de	**oo**-fu-ning
exhibition	tentoonstelling, de	ten-**tohn**-stel-ing
exit	uitgang, de	**uit**-CHang
expenses	onkosten, de	**on**-kos-tu
expensive	duur	duur
to expire (ticket, etc)	verlopen	ver-**loh**-pu
to explain	uitleggen	**uit**-leCH-CHu
express (train)	direct; snel	dee-**rect**; snel
extra	extra	**ex**-trah
an extra bed	een extra bed	un **ex**-trah bet
eye	oog, het	ohCH

F

English	Dutch	Pronunciation
face	gezicht, het	CHu-**ziCHt**
facilities	faciliteiten, de	fa-see-lee-**tei**-tu
to fail	falen	**fah**-lu
to faint	flauwvallen	**flow**-val-lu
fainted	flauwgevallen	**flow**-CHu-val-lu
fair (hair)	blond	blont
(just)	eerlijk	**ayr**-luk
fair (funfair)	kermis, de	**ker**-mis
(trade)	markt, de; beurs, de	markt; beurs
fake	namaak; nep	**nah**-mahk; nep
fall (autumn)	herfst, de; najaar, het	herfst; **nah**-yahr
to fall	vallen	**val**-lu
he/she has fallen	hij/zij is gevallen	hei/zei is CHu-**val**-lu
family	familie, de	fah-**mee**-lee
famous	beroemd	bu-**roomt**
far	ver	ver

English	Dutch	Pronunciation
is it far?	is het ver?	is ut ver?
fare (train, bus, etc)	prijs, de	preis
fashionable	modieus	moh-dee-**yeus**
fast	vlug; snel	vlueCH; snel
too fast	te vlug	tu vlueCH
to fasten (seatbelt)	vastmaken	**vast**-mah-ku
fat (substance)	vet, het	vet
(adj.)	dik	dik
father	vader, de	**vah**-der
fault (defect)	fout, de	fowt
it's not my fault	het is niet mijn fout	ut is neet mein fowt
favour	gunst, de	CHuenst
favourite	favoriet	fah-voh-**reet**
February	februari	fay-bruu-**ah**-ree
to feel	voelen	**voo**-lu
I don't feel well	ik voel me niet goed	ik vool mu neet CHoot
feet	voeten, de	**voo**-tu
female	vrouw, de	vrow
to fetch (to bring)	brengen	**breng**-u
(to go and get)	halen	**hah**-lu
fever	koorts, de	kohrts
few	enkele	**eng**-ku-lu
a few	enkele	**eng**-ku-lu
fiancé(e)	verloofde, de	ver-**lohf**-du
to fight	vechten	**veCH**-tu
to fill	vullen	**vuel**-lu
to fill in (form)	invullen	**in**-vuel-lu
fillet	filet, het	fee-**lay**
to find	vinden	**vin**-du
fine (to be paid)	boete, de	**boo**-tu
finger	vinger, de	**ving**-er
to finish	afmaken	**af**-mah-ku
finished	afgemaakt	**af**-CHu-mahkt
fire	vuur, het; brand, de	vuur; brant
fire alarm	brandalarm, het	**brant**-ah-larm
fire escape	brandtrap, de	**brant**-trap

fire extinguisher	brandblusser, de	**brant**-blues-ser
firm (company)	firma, de	**feer**-mah
first	eerste	**ayr**-stu
first aid	eerste hulp	**ayr**-stu huelp
first class (transport)	eerste klas	**ayr**-stu klas
first-class (top)	beste	**bes**-te
first name	voornaam, de	**vohr**-nahm
fish	vis, de	vis
to fish	vissen	**vis**-su
to go fishing	gaan vissen	CHahn **vis**-su
to fit (clothes)	passen	**pas**-su
it doesn't fit me	het past me niet	ut past mu neet
fit (seizure)	toeval, de	**too**-val
to fix	maken	**mah**-ku
can you fix it?	kunt u het maken?	kuent uu ut **mah**-ku?
fizzy	bruisend; met prik	**brui**-sunt; met prik
Flanders	Vlaanderen	**vlahn**-du-ru
flash (for camera)	flits, de	flits
flat (apartment)	flat, de	flet
flat	plat	plat
(battery)	leeg	layCH
flat tyre	lekke band, de	**lek**-ku bant
flavour	smaak, de	smahk
which flavour?	welke smaak?	**wel**-ku smahk?
Flemish	Vlaams	vlahms
flesh	vlees, het	vlays
flight	vlucht, de	vlueCHt
floor	vloer, de	vloor
(storey)	verdieping, de	ver-**dee**-ping
which floor?	welke verdieping?	**wel**-ku ver-**dee**-ping?
ground floor	begane grond, de	bu-**CHah**-nu CHront
first floor	eerste verdieping, de	**ayr**-stu ver-ver-**dee**-ping
flower	bloem, de	bloom

flu	griep, de	CHreep
to fly	vliegen	**vlee**-CHu
fog	mist, de	mist
foggy	mistig	**mis**-tiCH
to follow	volgen	**vol**-CHu
food	eten, het	**ay**-tu
food poisoning	voedselvergiftiging, de	**voot**-sel-ver-**CHif**-ti-CHing
foot (human)	voet, de;	voot;
(animal)	poot, de	poht
on foot	lopend	**loh**-punt
football	voetbal, het	**voot**-bal
for	voor	vohr
for me	voor mij	vohr mei
for you	voor jou	vohr yow
for him/her	voor hem/haar	vohr hem/hahr
forbidden	verboden	ver-**boh**-du
foreign	buitenlands	**bui**-tu-lants
foreigner	buitenlander, de	**bui**-tu-lan-der
forever	altijd	al-**teit**
to forget	vergeten	ver-**CHay**-tu

fork	vork, de	vork
form (document)	formulier, het	for-muu-**leer**
fortnight	twee weken	tway **way**-ku
forward(s)	voorwaarts	**vohr**-wahrts
fracture	breuk, de	breuk
fragile	breekbaar	**brayk**-bahr
France	Frankrijk	**frank**-reik
free (not occupied)	vrij	vrei
(costing nothing)	gratis	**CHrah**-tis
French	Frans	frans
French beans	sperziebonen, de	**sper**-zee-boh-nu
French fries	patat (patates frites), de	pa-**tat** (pa-**tat** freet)
frequent	frequent	fre-**kwent**
fresh	vers	vers
Friday	vrijdag	**vrei**-daCH
fried	gebakken	CHu-**bak**-ku
friend	vriend, de	vreent
friendly	vriendelijk	**vreen**-du-luk
from	van; uit	van; uit

English	Dutch	Pronunciation
from England	uit Engeland	uit **eng**-u-lant
front: *in front of*	voor	vohr
fruit	fruit, het	frowt
fruit juice	fruitsap, het	**frowt**-sap
to fry	bakken	**bak**-ku
fuel	brandstof, de	**brant**-stof
full	vol	vol
full board	vol pension	vol pen-**shon**
fun	plezier, het	plu-**zeer**
funny	grappig	**CHrap**-piCH
(strange)	vreemd	vraymt
furnished	gemeubileerd	CHu-meu-bee-**layrt**
future	toekomst, de	**too**-komst

G

English	Dutch	Pronunciation
gallery	galerie, de	CHah-lu-**ree**
game	spel, het	spel
(animal)	wild, het	wilt
garage	garage, de	CHah-**rah**-shu
garden	tuin, de	tuin
garlic	knoflook, de	**knof**-lohk
gate (airport)	uitgang, de	**uit**-CHang
gay (person)	homo, de/ lesbienne, de	**hoh**-moh/ les-bee-**en**-nu
gents (toilet)	heren	**hayr**-ru
genuine (leather, antique etc)	echt	eCHt
German	Duits	duits
Germany	Duitsland	**duits**-lant
to get (to obtain)	krijgen	**krei**-CHu
(to receive)	ontvangen	ont-**vang**-u
(to fetch)	halen	**hah**-lu
to get in/on (vehicle)	instappen	**in**-stap-pu
to get off	uitgaan	**uit**-CHahn
gift	cadeau, het	kah-**doh**
gift shop	cadeauwinkel, de	kah-**doh**-wing-kel
girl	meisje, het	**mei**-shu
girlfriend	vriendin, de	vreen-**din**

to give	geven	**CHay**-vu
to give back	teruggeven	tu-**rueCH**-CHay-vu
glass	glas, het	CHlas
a glass of water	een glas water	un CHlas **wah**-ter
glasses	bril, de	bril
to go	gaan	CHahn
I'm going to...	ik ga naar...	ik CHah nahr...
we're going to...	we gaan naar...	wu CHahn nahr...
to go back	teruggaan	tu-**rueCH**-CHahn
to go in	ingaan	**in**-CHahn
to go out	uitgaan	**uit**-CHahn
good	goed	CHoot
very good	zeer goed	zayr CHoot
good afternoon	goedemiddag	CHoo-du-**mid**-daCH
goodbye	dag; tot ziens	daCH; tot zeens
good evening	goedenavond	CHoo-dun-**ah**-vont
good morning	goedemorgen	CHoo-du-**mor**-CHun
good night	goedenacht;	CHoo-du-**naCHt**;
	welterusten	**wel**-tu-rues-tu
gram	gram, het	CHram
grandchild	kleinkind, het	**klein**-kint
grandparents	grootouders, de	**CHroht**-ow-ders
grapes	druiven, de	**drui**-vu
greasy	vet	vet
great (big)	groot	CHroht
(wonderful)	fantastisch	fan-**tas**-tees
Great Britain	Groot Brittannië	CHroht brit-**an**-nee-yu
green	groen	CHroon
greengrocer	groentewinkel, de	**CHroon**-tu-wing-kel
greetings card	wenskaart, de	**wens**-kahrt
grey	grijs	CHreis

grilled	gegrild	CHu-**CHrilt**
grocer	kruidenier, de	krui-du-**neer**
ground floor	begane grond, de	bu-**CHah**-nu CHront
group	groep, de	CHroop
guest	gast, de	CHast
guesthouse	pension, het	pen-**shon**
guide	gids, de	CHits
guidebook	handleiding, de	**hant**-lei-ding
guided tour	rondleiding, de	**ront**-lei-ding

H

hair	haar, het	hahr
hairdresser	kapper, de	**kap**-per
half	half	half
a half bottle of	een halve fles	un **hal**-vu fles
half an hour	een half uur	un half uur
half board	half pension	half pen-**shon**
ham	ham, de	ham
hand	hand, de	hant
handbag	handtas, de	**hant**-tas
handicapped (person)	gehandicapte; invalide	CHu-**han**-dee-cap-tu; in-va-**lee**-du
handkerchief	zakdoek, de	**zak**-dook
handlebars	stuur, het	stuur
hand luggage	handbagage, de	hant-bah-**CHah**-shu
hand-made	handgemaakt	**hant**-CHu-mahkt
handsome	mooi	**moh**-ee
to happen	gebeuren	CHu-**beu**-ru
what happened?	wat is er gebeurd?	wat is er CHu-**beurt**?
happy	gelukkig	CHu-**luek**-kiCH
happy birthday!	gefeliciteerd met je verjaardag!	CHu-**fay**-lee-see-**tayrt** met yu ver-**yahr**-daCH!
harbour	haven, de	**hah**-vu
hard	hard	hart
hard (difficult)	moeilijk	m**oo**-ee-luk

to have	hebben	**heb**-bu
I have...	ik heb...	ik heb...
I don't have...	ik heb niet/ geen...	ik heb neet/ CHayn...
we have...	we hebben...	wu **heb**-bu...
we don't have...	we hebben niet/ geen...	wu **heb**-bu neet/ CHayn...
do you have...?	heb je...?	heb yu...?
to have to	moeten	**moot**-tu
hay fever	hooikoorts, de	**hoy**-kohrts
he	hij	hei
head (person, horse)	hoofd, het	hohft
(animal)	kop, het	kop
headache	hoofdpijn, de	**hohft**-pein
I have a headache	ik heb hoofdpijn	ik heb **hohft**-pein
health	gezondheid, de	CHu-**zont**-heit
health food shop I	reformwinkel, de	ru-**form**-wing-kel
healthy	gezond	CHu-**zont**
to hear	horen	**hoh**-ru
heart	hart, het	hart
to heat up	opwarmen	**op**-war-mu
heating	verwarming, de	ver-**war**-ming
heavy	zwaar	zwahr
height	hoogte, de	**hohCH**-tu
hello	hallo	hal-**loh**
help	hulp, de	huelp
help!	help!	help!
to help	helpen	**hel**-pu
can you help me?	kunt u me helpen?	kuent uu mu **hel**-pu?
her	haar	hahr
here	hier	heer
here is...	hier is...	heer is...
here is my passport	hier is mijn paspoort	heer is mein **pas**-pohrt
hi!	hoi!	hoy!
to hide	verbergen	ver-**ber**-CHu
high	hoog	hohCH
high chair	kinderstoel	**kin**-der-stool

English	Dutch	Pronunciation
him	hem	hem
hire	huur, de	huur
car hire	autoverhuur, de	**ow**-toh-ver-huur
bike hire	fietsverhuur, de	**feets**-ver-huur
to hire	huren	**huu**-ru
hire car	huurauto, de	**huur**-ow-toh
his	zijn	zein
historic	historisch	his-**toh**-rees
hobby	hobby, de	**hob**-bee
to hold (to contain)	bevatten	bu-**vat**-tu
holiday (public holiday)	vakantie, de	va-**kan**-see
	vrije dag	**vrei**-yu daCH
on holiday	op vakantie	op va-**kan**-see
home	huis, het	huis
at home	thuis	tuis
to go home	naar huis gaan	nahr huis CHahn
homeopathic	homeopathisch	hoh-may-oh-**pah**-tees
homosexual	homoseksueel	hoh-moh-seks-uu-**ayl**

English	Dutch	Pronunciation
honest	eerlijk	**ayr**-luk
to hope	hopen	**hoh**-pu
I hope so	ik hoop het	ik hohp ut
I hope not	ik hoop niet	ik hohp neet
hors d'œuvre	voorgerecht, het	**vohr**-CHu-reCHt
hospital	ziekenhuis, het	**zee**-ku-huis
hot	heet	hayt
I'm hot	ik heb het heet	ik heb ut hayt
it's hot	het is warm	ut is warm
hot chocolate	warme chocolademelk, de	**war**-mu shoh-coh-**lah**-du-melk
hotel	hotel, het	hoh-**tel**
hour	uur, het	uur
half an hour	half uur	half uur
half past seven (time)	half acht	half aCHt
1 hour	een uur	ayn uur
2 hours	twee uur	tway uur
house	huis, het	huis

house wine	huiswijn, de	**huis**-wein
how	hoe	hoo
how much?	hoeveel?	**hoo**-vayl?
how many?	hoeveel?	**hoo**-vayl?
how are you?	hoe gaat het?	hoo CHaht ut?
hungry: *I am hungry*	ik heb honger	ik heb **hong**-er
hurry: *I'm in a hurry*	ik heb haast	ik heb hahst
to hurt	pijn doen	pein doon
that hurts	dat doet pijn	dat doot pein
my back hurts	mijn rug doet pijn	mein rueCH doot pein
husband	echtgenoot, de	**eCHt**-CHu-noht

I

I	ik	ik
ice	ijs, het	eis
ice cream	ijs, het	eis
iced tea	ijsthee, de	**eis**-tay
ice lolly	ijslolly, de	**eis**-lolly
idea	idee, het	ee-**day**
identity card	identiteitskaart, de	ee-den-tee-**teits**-kahrt
if	als; wanneer	als; wan-**nayr**
ill	ziek	zeek
I'm ill	ik ben ziek	ik ben zeek
illness	ziekte, de	**zeek**-tu
immediately	onmiddellijk	on-**mid**-du-luk
important	belangrijk	bu-**lang**-reik
impossible	onmogelijk	on-**moh**-CHu-luk
to improve	verbeteren	ver-**bay**-tu-ru
in	in	in
in front of	voor	vohr
included	inclusief	in-cluu-**seef**
inconvenient	lastig	**las**-tiCH
to increase	toenemen	**too**-nay-mu
indigestion	indigestie, de	in-dee-**CHes**-tee
indoors	binnen	**bin**-nu
infection	infectie, de	in-**fek**-see
informal	informeel	in-for-**mayl**

information	informatie, de	in-for-**mah**-see
ingredient	ingrediënt, het	in-CHray-dee-**yent**
to injure	verwonden	ver-**won**-du
injured	gewond	CHu-**wont**
in-law	schoon-	sCHohn-
mother-in-law etc.	schoonmoeder	**sCHohn**-moo-der
except:		
brother-in-law	zwager, de	**zwah**-CHer
inner tube	binnenband, de	**bin**-nu-bant
inquiries	inlichtingen, de	**in**-liCH-ting-u
insect	insect, het	in-**sect**
inside	binnen	**bin**-nu
instant coffee	oploskoffie, de	op-los-**kof**-fee
instead of	in plaats van	in plahts van
insurance	verzekering, de	ver-**zay**-ku-ring
insurance certificate	verzekerings-bewijs, het	ver-**zay**-ku-rings-bu-weis
insured: ***to be insured***	verzekerd zijn	ver-**zay**-kert zein
interesting	interessant	in-ter-es-**sant**
internet	internet, het	**in**ternet
internet café	internet café, het	**in**ternet ca-**fay**
international	internationaal	in-ter-nah-shee-oh-**nahl**
into	in	in
to introduce (someone to someone)	voorstellen	**vohr**-stel-lu
invitation	uitnodiging, de	**uit**-noh-di-CHing
to invite	uitnodigen	**uit**-noh-di-CHu
Ireland	Ierland	**eer**-lant
Irish	Iers	eers
iron (for clothes)	strijkijzer, het	**streik**-ei-zer
island	eiland, het	**ei**-lant
it	het	ut
to itch	jeuken	**yeu**-ku

J

jacket	jas, de	yas
jam	jam, de	shem

English	Dutch	Pronunciation
January	januari	yah-nuu-**ah**-ree
jar	pot, de	pot
jealous	jaloers	yah-**loors**
jeans	spijkerbroek, de	**spei**-ker-brook
jeweller	juwelier, de	yuu-wu-**leer**
jewellery	sieraden	see-**rah**-du
Jewish	joods	yohts
job	baan, de	bahn
to join (club)	lid worden	lit **wor**-du
to joke	grappen maken	**CHrap**-pu **mah**-ku
journalist	journalist, de	shoor-nah-**list**
journey	reis, de	reis
juice	sap, het	sap
July	juli	**yuu**-lee
to jump	springen	**spring**-u
junction	kruising, de	**krui**-sing
June	juni	**yuu**-nee
just	net;	net;
(only)	slechts	sleCHts
just two	slechts twee	sleCHts tway
I've just arrived	ik ben net aangekomen	ik ben net **ahn**-CHu-koh-mu

K

English	Dutch	Pronunciation
to keep	houden	how-du
keep the change!	houd het wisselgeld maar!	howt ut **wis**-sel-CHelt mahr!
key	sleutel, de	**sleu**-tel
car key	autosleutel, de	**ow**-toh-sleu-tel
to kill	doden	**doh**-du
kilo	kilo, de	**kee**-loh
kilogram	kilogram, de	**kee**-loh-CHram
kilometre	kilometer, de	**kee**-loh-may-ter
kind (adj.)	aardig	**ahr**-diCH
(sort)	soort, het	sohrt
kiosk	kiosk, de	kee-**osk**
to kiss	kussen; zoenen	**kues**-su; **zoon**-nu
to knock	kloppen	**klop**-pu
to know (have knowledge of)	weten	**way**-tu
(person, place)	kennen	**ken**-nu

English	Dutch	Pronunciation
I don't know	ik weet het niet	ik wayt ut neet
to know (how to do something)	kunnen	**kuen**-nu
I know how to swim	ik kan zwemmen	ik kan **zwem**-mu
kosher	kosjer	**koh**-sher

L

English	Dutch	Pronunciation
ladies (toilet)	dames	**dah**-mus
lady	vrouw, de	vrow
lager (pils)	bier, het	beer
lamb	lam, het	lam
lamp	lamp, de	lamp
land	land, het	lant
to land	landen	**lan**-du
language	taal, de	tahl
large	groot	CHroht
last	laatst	lahtst
the last bus	de laatste bus	du **laht**-stu bues
last night	gisternacht	**CHis**-ter-naCHt
last week	vorige week	**vor**-ri-CHu wayk
last year	vorig jaar	**vor**-riCH yahr
late	laat	laht
sorry we are late	sorry, we zijn te laat	sorry, wu zein tu laht
later	later	**lah**-ter
to laugh	lachen	**laCH**-u
lavatory	toilet, het	twa-**let**
laxative	laxeermiddel, het	lak-**sayr**-mid-del
lazy	lui	lui
to learn	leren	**layr**-ru
leather	leer, het	layr
to leave (leave behind)	achterlaten	**aCH**-ter-lah-tu
(train, bus, etc)	vertrekken	ver-**trek**-ku
when does the train leave?	hoe laat vertrekt de trein?	hoo laht ver-**trekt** du trein?
left	links	links
on/to the left	aan de linkerkant	ahn du **ling**-ker-kant
turn left	ga linksaf	CHah **link**-saf

English	Dutch	Pronunciation
left luggage (office)	bagagedepot, het	bah-**CHah**-shu-du-poh
left luggage locker	bagagekluis, de	bah-**CHah**-shu-kluis
leg	been, het	bayn
lemon	citroen, de	see-**troon**
lemonade	limonade, de	lee-moh-**nah**-du
to lend	lenen	**leh**-nu
length	lengte, de	**leng**-tu
lens (of camera)	lens, de	lens
lenses (contact lenses)	lenzen, de	**len**-zu
less	minder	**min**-der
less than	minder dan	**min**-der dan
lesson	les, de	les
to let (allow)	toestaan	**too**-stahn
(lease)	verhuren	ver-**huu**-ru
letter	brief, de	breef
licence	vergunning, de	ver-**CHuen**-ning
(driving)	rijbewijs, het	**rei**-bu-weis
to lie	liegen	**lee**-CHu
lie (untruth)	leugen, de	**leu**-CHun
to lie down	(gaan) liggen; rusten	(CHahn) **liCH**-u; **rues**-tu
lift (elevator)	lift, de	lift
light (not heavy/not dark)	licht	liCHt
do you have a light	heb je een vuurtje	heb yu un **vuur**-chu
like	als	als
to like (food)	lekker vinden	**lek**-ker **vin**-du
(person, place)	houden van	**how**-du van
I like coffee	ik vind koffie lekker	ik vint **kof**-fee **lek**-ker
I don't like...	ik hou niet van...	ik how neet van...
I'd like to...	ik wil...	ik wil...
we'd like to...	we willen...	wu **wil**-lu...
liqueur	likeur, de	lee-**keur**
liquorice	drop, de	drop
list	lijst, de	leist
to listen to	luisteren naar	**luis**-tu-ru nahr
litre	liter	**lee**-ter

English	Dutch	Pronunciation
a litre of milk	een liter melk	un **lee**-ter melk
little	klein	klein
a little...	een klein beetje...	un klein **bay**-chu...
to live	wonen; leven	**woh**-nu; **lay**-vu
I live in Edinburgh	ik woon in Edinburg	ik wohn in **ay**-din-buerCH
to lock	sluiten	**slui**-tu
locker (luggage)	kluis, de	kluis
London	Londen	**lon**-du
long	lang	lang
to look at	kijken naar	**kei**-ku nahr
to look for	zoeken	**zoo**-ku
to lose	verliezen	ver-**lee**-zu
lost	verloren	ver-**loh**-ru
I have lost my wallet	ik heb mijn portefeuille verloren	ik heb mein por-tu-**feu**-yu ver-**loh**-ru
I am lost	ik ben verdwaald	ik ben ver-**dwahlt**
lost property office (sign)	gevonden voorwerpen	CHu-**von**-du **vohr**-wer-pu
lot: *a lot* (much, many)	veel	vayl
loud (noisy)	luid	luit
lounge (in hotel)	lounge, de	lounge
(in airport)	hal, de	hal
to love	houden van	**how**-du van
I love swimming	ik hou van zwemmen	ik how van **zwem**-mu
I love you	ik hou van jou	ik how van yow
lovely	mooi	**moh**-ee
low	laag	lahCH
low-fat	met laag vetgehalte	met lahCH **vet**-CHu-hal-tu
luck	geluk, het	CHu-**luek**
lucky	gelukkig	CHu-**luek**-kiCH
luggage	bagage, de	bah-**CHah**-shu
luggage trolley	bagagewagentje, het	bah-**CHah**-shu-**wah**-CHun-chu
lunch	lunch, de	lunch

luxury luxe, de **luuk**-su

M

machine machine, de ma-**shee**-nu
mad (insane) gek CHek
(angry) boos bohs
magazine blad, het blat
maid kamermeisje, het **kah**-mer-mei-shu
mail post, de post
main course (of meal) hoofdgerecht, het **hohft**-CHu-reCHt
to make (generally) maken **mah**-ku
(meal) klaarmaken **klahr**-mah-ku
male mannelijk **man**-nu-luk
man man, de man
map kaart, de kahrt
March maart mahrt
margarine margarine mar-CHah-**ree**-nu
market markt, de markt
where is the market? waar is de markt? wahr is de markt?
when is the market? wanneer is er markt? wan-**nayr** is er markt?
marmalade marmelade, de mar-mu-**lah**-du
married getrouwd CHu-**trowt**
I'm married ik ben getrouwd ik ben CHu-**trowt**
are you married? ben je getrouwd? ben yu CHu-**trowt**?
marry: ***to get married*** trouwen **trow**-wu
to matter: ***it doesn't matter*** het geeft niet ut CHayft neet
what's the matter? wat is er? wat is er?
matches lucifers, de **luu**-see-fers
May mei mei
me mij mei
meal maaltijd, de **mahl**-teit
to mean betekenen bu-**tay**-ku-nu

English	Dutch	Pronunciation
what does this mean?	wat betekent dit?	wat bu-**tay**-kent dit?
to measure	meten	**may**-tu
meat	vlees, het	vlays
I don't eat meat	ik eet geen vlees	ik ayt CHayn vlays
medicine	medicijn, het	may-dee-**sein**
to meet	ontmoeten	ont-**moot**-tu
pleased to meet you	aangenaam kennis te maken	**ahn**-CHu-nahm **ken**-nis tu **mah**-ku
to melt	smelten	**smel**-tu
memory	geheugen, het	CHu-**heu**-CHu
(thing remembered)	herinnering, de	her-**in**-nu-ring
men	mannen, de	**man**-nu
to mend	repareren	ray-pah-**rayr**-ru
menu	menu, het	mu-**nuu**
set menu	dagmenu, het	**daCH**-me-nuu
message	boodschap, de	**boht**-sCHap
metre	meter, de	**may**-ter
metro (underground)	metro, de	**may**-troh
midday	middag, de; twaalf uur	**mid**-daCH; twahlf uur
at midday	om twaalf uur	om twahlf uur
middle	middel	**mid**-del
midnight	middernacht	**mid**-der-naCHt
at midnight	om middernacht	om **mid**-der-naCHt
mild	mild	milt
milk	melk, de	melk
fresh milk	verse melk, de	**ver**-su melk
with milk	met melk	met melk
without milk	zonder melk	**zon**-der melk
millimetre	millimeter, de	**mee**-lee-**may**-ter
mind	verstand, het	ver-**stant**
to mind (take care of)	zorgen voor	**zor**-CHu vohr
(object to)	bezwaren; hebben tegen	bu-**zwah**-ru **heb**-bu **tay**-CHu

do you mind if...?	vind je het goed als...?	vint yu ut CHoot als...?
I don't mind	ik vind het niet erg	ik vint ut neet erCH
mineral water	mineraal water, het	mee-nu-**rahl**-wah-ter
minimum	minimum, het	**mee**-nee-muem
minute	minuut, de	mee-**nuut**
mirror	spiegel, de	**spee**-CHel
to misbehave	misdragen	mis-**drah**-CHu
Miss...	Mejuffrouw...	mu-**yuef**-frow...
to miss (train, etc)	missen	**mis**-su
missing (lost)	vermist	ver-**mist**
mistake	fout, de	fowt
mobile phone	mobiele telefoon, de; gsm, de	moh-**bee**-lu **tay**-lu-fohn; **CHay**-es-em
modern	modern	moh-**dern**
moment	moment, het	moh-**ment**
just a moment	een ogenblik alstublieft	un **oh**-CHun-blik als-tuu-**bleeft**

Monday	maandag	**mahn**-daCH
money	geld, het	CHelt
I have no money	ik heb geen geld	ik heb CHayn CHelt
month	maand, de	mahnt
this month	deze maand	**day**-zu mahnt
last month	vorige maand	**vor**-ri-CHu mahnt
next month	volgende maand	**vol**-CHun-du mahnt
more	meer	mayr
more than three	meer dan drie	mayr dan dree
morning	ochtend, de; morgen, de	**oCH**-tunt; **mor**-CHun
in the morning	's ochtends	**soCH**-tunts
this morning	vanochtend	van-**oCH**-tunt
tomorrow morning	morgenochtend	**mor**-CHun-oCH-tunt
morning-after pill	morning-after-pil, de	morning-after-pil

most	meest	mayst
mother	moeder, de	**moo**-der
motor	motor, de	**moh**-tor
motorbike	motorfiets; bromfiets, de	**moh**-tor-feets; **brom**-feets
motorway	autoweg, de	**ow**-toh-weCH
mouth	mond, de	mont
to move	bewegen	bu-**way**-Chu
it isn't moving	het beweegt niet	ut bu-**wayCHt** neet
movie	film, de	film
Mr	Meneer *(abbr. in address* Dhr*)*	mu-**nayr**
Mrs/Ms	Mevrouw *(abbr.* Mevr*)*	mu-**vrow**
much	veel	vayl
too much	teveel	tu-**vayl**
muddy	modderig	**mod**-der-iCH
mugging	beroving	bu-**roh**-ving
muscle	spier, de	speer
museum	museum, het	muu-**say**-uem
music	muziek, de	muu-**seek**
must (to have to)	moeten	**moot**-tu
I must	ik moet	ik moot
we must	we moeten	wu **moot**-tu
I mustn't	ik moet niet	ik moot neet
we mustn't	we moeten niet	we **moot**-tu neet
my	mijn	mein

N

name	naam, de	nahm
my name is...	mijn naam is...; ik heet...	mein nahm is...; ik hayt...
what's your name?	wat is jouw naam?	wat is yow nahm?
nappy	luier, de	**lui**-yer
narrow	nauw	now
national	nationaal	nah-shee-oh-**nahl**
nationality	nationaliteit, de	nah-shee-oh-nah-lee-**teit**
natural	natuurlijk	na-**tuur**-luk

nature	natuur, de	na-**tuur**
near	bij	bei
near the bank	bij de bank	bei du bank
is it near?	is het dichtbij?	is ut diCHt-**bei**?
necessary	noodzakelijk	noht-**zah**-ku-luk
to need	nodig hebben;	**noh**-diCH **heb**-bu;
	moeten	**moot**-tu
I need...	ik heb ... nodig	ik heb ... **noh**-diCH
we need...	wij hebben... nodig	wu **heb**-bu... **noh**-diCH
never	nooit	**noh**-eet
I never drink wine	ik drink nooit wijn	ik drink **noh**-eet wein
new	nieuw	**nee**-yoo
news	nieuws, het	**nee**-yoos
(TV)	journaal, het	shoor-**nahl**
newspaper	krant, de	krant
newsstand	kiosk, de	kee-**osk**
New Year	Nieuwjaar	**nee**-yoo-yahr

Happy New Year!	Gelukkig Nieuwjaar!	CHu-**luek**-kiCH **nee**-yoo-yahr!
New Year's Eve	Oudejaarsavond	**ow**-du-yahrs-ah-vont
New Zealand	Nieuw Zeeland	**nee**-yoo **zay**-lant
next	volgende	**vol**-CHun-du
next to	naast	nahst
next week	volgende week	**vol**-CHun-du wayk
the next stop	de volgende halte	du **vol**-CHun-du **hal**-tu
nice (person)	aardig	**ahr**-diCH
(holiday, place)	leuk	leuk
night	nacht, de	naCHt
at night	's nachts	snaCHts
last night	vorige nacht	**vor**-ri-CHu naCHt
tonight	vannacht	van-**naCHt**
no	nee	nay

English	Dutch	Pronunciation
no entry	geen toegang	CHayn **too**-CHang
no smoking	niet roken	neet **roh**-ku
no thanks	nee, dank je	nay, dank yu
no (without)	zonder	**zon**-der
nobody	niemand	**nee**-mant
noise	geluid, het	CHu-**luit**
noisy	lawaaierig	lah-**wah**-yu-riCH
non-alcoholic	alcoholvrij	al-coh-hol-**vrei**
none	geen	CHayn
north	noord	nohrt
Northern Ireland	Noord Ierland	nohrd **eer**-lant
North Sea	Noordzee, de	**nohrd**-zay
nose	neus, de	neus
not	niet	neet
nothing	niets	neets
nothing else	niets anders	neets **an**-ders
now	nu	nuu
nowhere	nergens	**ner**-Chuns

English	Dutch	Pronunciation
nudist beach	naaktstrand, het	**nahkt**-strant
number	nummer, het	**nuem**-mer

O

English	Dutch	Pronunciation
to obtain	krijgen	**krei**-CHu
October	oktober	ok-**toh**-ber
odd (number)	oneven	on-**ay**-vu
of	van	van
a bottle of water	een fles water	un fles **wah**-ter
made of...	gemaakt van...	CHu-**mahkt** van...
off (radio, engine, etc)	uit	uit
(milk, food, etc)	bedorven	bu-**dor**-vu
office	kantoor, het	kan-**tohr**
often	vaak	vahk
how often?	hoe vaak?	hoo vahk?
old	oud	owt
how old are you?	hoe oud ben je?	hoo owt ben yu?

English	Dutch	Pronunciation
I'm... years old	ik ben...	ik ben...
on (light, TV, engine)	aan	ahn
on	op	op
on the table	op de tafel	op du **tah**-fel
on time	op tijd	op teit
once	eens	ayns
at once	onmiddelijk	on-**mid**-du-luk
onion	ui, de	ui
only	alleen	al-**layn**
(adj)	enige	**ay**-ni-CHu
open	open	**oh**-pun
to open	openen	**oh**-pu-nu
opposite:		
opposite (to)	tegenover	tay-CHun-**oh**-ver
or	of	of
orange (fruit)	sinaasappel, de	**see**-nahs-ap-pel
(colour)	oranje	oh-**ran**-yu
orange juice	sinaasappelsap, het	**see**-nahs-ap-pel-sap
to order (in restaurant)	bestellen	bu-**stel**-lu
organic	biologisch	bee-oh-**loh**-CHees
to organize	organiseren	or-CHah-nee-**sayr**-ru
other: ***the other one***	de andere	**an**-du-ru
our	ons; onze	ons; **on**-zu
out (light)	uit	uit
he's out	hij is er niet	hei is er neet
out of order	buiten dienst	**bui**-tu deenst
over (on top of)	boven	**boh**-vu
overdone (food)	overgaar	**oh**-ver-CHahr

P

English	Dutch	Pronunciation
package	pakket, het	pak-**ket**
package tour	geheel verzorgde reis, de	CHu-**hayl** ver-**zorCH**-du reis
page	bladzijde, de	**blat**-zei-du
paid	betaald	bu-**tahlt**
pain	pijn, de	pein
painful	pijnlijk	**pein**-luk

English	Dutch	Pronunciation
painkiller	pijnstiller, de	**pein**-stil-ler
painting	schilderij, het	sCHil-du-**rei**
pair	paar, het	pahr
palace	paleis, het	pah-**leis**
pancake	pannenkoek, de	**pan**-nu-kook
panty liner	inlegkruisje, het	**in**-leCH-krui-shu
paper	papier, het	pah-**peer**
(newspaper)	krant, de	krant
parcel	pakket, het	pak-**ket**
pardon?	pardon?	par-**don**?
I beg your pardon!	het spijt me!	ut speit mu!
parents	ouders, de	**ow**-ders
park	park, het	park
to park	parkeren	par-**kayr**-ru
part	deel, het	dayl
partner	partner, de	**part**-ner
party (celebration)	feest, het	fayst
passenger	passagier, de	**pas**-sa-sheer
passport	paspoort, het	**pas**-pohrt
pastry (dough)	deeg	dayCH
(cake)	gebak, het	CHu-**bak**
to pay	betalen	bu-**tah**-lu
I'd like to pay	ik wil graag betalen	ik wil CHrahCH bu-**tah**-lu
where do I pay?	waar kan ik betalen?	wahr kan ik bu-**tah**-lu?
payment	betaling, de	bu-**tah**-ling
payphone	telefooncel, de	**tay**-lu-fohn-sell
peace	vrede, de	**vray**-du
peach	perzik, de	**per**-zik
peanut	pinda, de	**pin**-dah
peanut allergy	allergisch voor pinda's	al-**ler**-CHees vohr **pin**-dahs
peanut butter	pindakaas, de	**pin**-dah-kahs
pear	peer, de	payr
peas	erwten, de	**er**-tu
to pee	plassen	**plas**-su
to peel (fruit)	schillen	**sCHil**-lu
pen	pen, de	pen
pensioner	bejaarde, de	bu-**yahr**-de

English	Dutch	Pronunciation
people	mensen, de	**men**-su
pepper (spice)	peper, de	**pay**-per
(vegetable)	paprika, de	**pah**-pree-kah
per	per	per
per day	per dag	per daCH
per week	per week	per wayk
per person	per persoon	per per-**sohn**
performance	uitvoering, de	**uit**-voor-ring
perhaps	misschien	mis-**CHeen**
person	persoon, de	per-**sohn**
petrol	benzine, de	ben-**zee**-nu
unleaded petrol	loodvrije benzine, de	**loht**-vrei-yu ben-**zee**-nu
petrol station	benzinestation, het	ben-**zee**-nu-sta-**shon**
pharmacy	apotheek, de	ah-poh-**tayk**
phone	*see telephone*	
to phone	opbellen	**op**-bel-lu
to photocopy	kopiëren	koh-pee-**yayr**-ru
photograph	foto, de	**foh**-toh
to take a photograph	een foto maken	un **foh**-toh **mah**-ku
phrasebook	taalgids, de	**tahl**-CHits
to pick	kiezen	**kee**-zu
piece	stuk, het	stuek
pillow	kussen, het	**kues**-su
pink	roze	**roh**-zu
pity: ***what a pity!***	wat jammer!	wat **yam**-mer!
pizza	pizza, de	**pit**-zah
place	plaats, de	plahts
place of birth	geboorteplaats, de	CHu-**bohr**-tu-plahts
plain (ordinary)	gewoon;	CHu-**wohn**;
(yoghurt, etc)	naturel	nah-tuu-**rel**
(obvious)	duidelijk	**dui**-du-luk
to plan	plannen	**plan**-nu
plane	vliegtuig, het	**vleeCH**-tuiCH
plaster (sticking)	pleister, de	**pleis**-ter
(for broken limb)	gips, het	CHips

platform (railway)	perron, het; spoor, het	per-**ron**; spohr
which platform?	welk spoor?	welk spohr?
play (at theatre)	toneelstuk, het	toh-**nayl**-stuk
to play	spelen	**spay**-lu
pleasant	plezierig	plu-**zeer**-riCH
please (formal)	alstublieft	als-tuu-**bleeft**
(informal)	alsjeblieft	als-yu-**bleeft**
pleased:	aangenaam	**ahn**-CHu-nahm
pleased to meet you	kennis te maken	**ken**-nis tu **mah**-ku
plum	pruim, de	pruim
poached	gepocheerd	CHu-po-**shayrt**
pocket	zak, de	zak
poisonous	vergiftig	ver-**CHif**-tiCH
police	politie, de	poh-**lee**-tsee
police station	politiebureau, het	poh-**lee**-tsee-buu-**roh**
polluted	vervuild	ver-**vuilt**
pool	zwembad, het	**zwem**-bat
poor	arm	arm
pork	varkensvlees	**var**-kuns-vlays
possible	mogelijk	**moh**-CHu-luk
post: ***by post***	per post	per post
to post	versturen	ver-**stuu**-ru
post box	brievenbus, de	**bree**-vu-bues
postcard	briefkaart, de	**brief**-kahrt
post office	postkantoor, het	**post**-kan-tohr
to postpone	uitstellen	**uit**-stel-lu
potato	aardappel, de	**ahrd**-ap-pel
pound (money)	pond, het	pont
(weight)	pond, het (500 grams)	pont
to pour	schenken	**sCHeng**-ku
power (electricity)	stroom, de	strohm
prescription	voorschrift, het	**vohr**-sCHrift
present (gift)	cadeau, het	kah-**doh**
pretty	mooi	**moh**-ee
price	prijs, de	preis
price list	prijslijst, de	**preis**-leist

private	privé	pree-**vay**
probably	waarschijnlijk	wahr-**sCHein**-luk
problem	probleem, het	proh-**blaym**
no problem	geen probleem	CHayn proh-**blaym**
prohibited	verboden	ver-**boh**-du
to promise	beloven	bu-**loh**-vu
to pronounce	uitspreken	**uit**-spray-ku
how is this pronounced?	hoe wordt dit uitgesproken?	hoo wort dit **uit**-CHu-sproh-ku?
to provide	voorzien	**vohr**-zeen
public	openbaar	oh-pen-**bahr**
public holiday	nationale feestdag, de	nah-shee-oh-**nah**-lu **fayst**-daCH
to pull	trekken	**trek**-ku
purple	paars	pahrs
purse	portemonnee, de	**por**-tu-mon-nay
to push	duwen	**doo**-wu
to put	zetten	**zet**-tu

Q

quality	kwaliteit, de	kwa-lee-**teit**
quantity	hoeveelheid, de	hoo-**vayl**-heit
to quarrel	ruzie maken	**ruu**-zee **mah**-ku
quarter	kwart, het	kwart
(city)	kwartier, het	kwar-**teer**
question	vraag, de	vrahCH
queue	rij, de	rei
to queue	in de rij staan	in du rei stahn
quick	vlug	vlueCH
quiet (place)	rustig	**rues**-tiCH
a quiet room	een stille kamer	un **stil**-lu **kah**-mer
quite	nogal	noCH-**al**

R

radio	radio, de	**rah**-dee-oh
railway station	station, het	sta-**shon**
rain	regen	**ray**-CHu
it's raining	het regent	ut **ray**-CHunt
raincoat	regenjas, de	**ray**-CHun-yas

English	Dutch	Pronunciation
raped	verkracht	ver-**kraCHt**
rare (unique)	zeldzaam	**zelt**-zahm
(steak)	kort gebakken	kort CHu-**bak**-ku
raspberries	frambozen, de	fram-**boh**-zu
rate (price)	prijs, de	preis
rate of exchange	wisselkoers, de	**wis**-sel-koors
raw	rauw	row
razor	scheerapparaat, het	**sCHayr**-ap-pah-raht
razorblades	scheermesjes, de	**sCHayr**-mesh-us
to read	lezen	**lay**-zu
ready	klaar	klahr
real	echt	eCHt
receipt	bonnetje, het	**bon**-nut-chu
reception (desk)	receptie, de	ray-**sep**-see
to recognize	herkennen	her-**ken**-nu
to recommend	aanbevelen	ahn-bu-**vay**-lu
red	rood	roht
reduction	korting, de	**kor**-ting

English	Dutch	Pronunciation
to refer to	verwijzen naar	ver-**wei**-zu nahr
refund	terugbetaling, de	tu-**rueCH**-bu-**tah**-ling
to refuse	weigeren	**wei**-CHu-ru
regarding	betreffende	bu-**tref**-fun-du
region	regio, de	**ray**-CHee-oh
to register (at hotel)	inschrijven	**in**-sCHrei-vu
registration form	inschrijvings-formulier, het	**in**-sCHrei-vings-for-muu-**leer**
to reimburse	vergoeden	ver-**CHoo**-du
relationship	relatie, de	re-**lah**-tsee
relative (family)	familielid, het	fah-**mee**-lee-lit
to remain	blijven	**blei**-vu
to remember	herinneren	her-**rin**-nu-ru
I don't remember	ik herinner me niet	ik her-**rin**-ner mu neet
to remove	weghalen	**weCH**-hah-lu
repair	reparatie, de	ray-pah-**rah**-tsee
to repair	repareren	ray-pah-**rayr**-ru
to repeat	herhalen	her-**hah**-lu

English	Dutch	Pronunciation
to reply	antwoorden	**ant**-wohr-du
to report (crime)	aangifte doen	**ahn**-CHif-tu doon
request	verzoek, het	ver-**zook**
to request	verzoeken	ver-**zoo**-ku
reservation	reservering, de	ray-ser-**vayr**-ring
to reserve	reserveren	ray-ser-**vayr**-ru
reserved	gereserveerd	CHu-ray-ser-**vayrt**
rest (repose)	rust, de	ruest
(remainder)	rest, de	rest
to rest	rusten	**rues**-tu
restaurant	restaurant, het	res-toh-**rant**
retired	gepensioeneerd	CHu-pen-see-oh-**nayrt**
I'm retired	ik ben gepensioeneerd	ik ben CHu-pen-see-oh-**nayrt**
to return (to go back)	terug gaan	tu-**rueCH** CHahn
(to give something back)	terug geven	tu-**rueCH** **CHay**-vu
return ticket	retour, het	ru-**toor**
rice	rijst, de	reist
rich (person)	rijk	reik
(food)	machtig	**maCH**-tiCH
right (correct)	goed	CHoot
to be right	gelijk hebben	CHu-**leik** heb-bu
right (direction)	rechts	reCHts
on/to the right	aan de rechterkant	ahn du **reCH**-ter-kant
turn right	ga rechtsaf	CHah **reCHt**-saf
to ring	bellen	**bel**-lu
ring road	ringweg, de	**ring**-weCH
road	weg, de	weCH
road map	wegenkaart, de	**way**-CHun-kahrt
road sign	verkeersbord, het	ver-**kayrs**-bort
to roast	braden	**brah**-du
roll (bread)	broodje, het	**broht**-chu
Romanesque	Romaans	roh-**mahns**
room (in house, hotel)	kamer, de	**kah**-mer
(space)	ruimte, de	**ruim**-tu

double room	tweepersoons-kamer, de	**tway**-per-sohns-**kah**-mer
family room	familiekamer, de	fah-**mee**-lee-**kah**-mer
single room	eenpersoons-kamer, de	**ayn**-per-sohns-**kah**-mer
room number	kamernummer, het	**kah**-mer-**nuem**-mer
rose	roos, de	rohs
rosé wine	rosé	roh-**say**
round (shape)	rond	ront
row (line)	rij, de	rei
royal	koninklijk	**koh**-ning-kluk
to run	rennen	**ren**-nu

S

sad	droevig	**droo**-viCH
safe (for valuables)	kluis, de	kluis
safe	veilig	**vei**-liCH
is it safe?	is het veilig?	is ut **vei**-liCH?
safety	veiligheid, de	**vei**-liCH-heit
salad	salade, de	sa-**lah**-du
salad dressing	slasaus, de	**slah**-sows
salami	cervelaat, de	**ser**-vu-laht
sale(s)	(uit)verkoop, de	(uit)ver-**kohp**
salesman	verkoper, de	ver-**koh**-per
salt	zout, het	zowt
salty	zout	zowt
same	hetzelfde	ut-**zelf**-du
sand	zand, het	zant
sandwich	boterham, de	**boh**-ter-ham
toasted sandwich	tosti, de	**tos**-tee
sanitary towel	maandverband, het	**mahnt**-ver-bant
satellite TV	satelliet TV, de	sah-tu-**leet** tay-**vay**
Saturday	zaterdag	**zah**-ter-daCH
sauce	saus, de	sows
sausage	worst, de	worst
savoury	hartig	**har**-tiCH

to say	zeggen	**zeCH**-u
school	school, de	sCHohl
Scot	Schot, de	sCHot
Scotland	Schotland	**sCHot**-lant
Scottish	Schots	sCHots
sculpture	beeld, het	baylt
sea	zee, de	zay
seafood	zeevruchten, de	**zay**-vrueCH-tu
to search for	zoeken naar	**zoo**-ku nahr
seasick	zeeziek	**zay**-zeek
seaside	kust, de	kuest
at the seaside	aan de kust	ahn du kuest
season (of year)	seizoen, het	sei-**zoon**
in season	-tijd	-teit
seasoning	kruiden, de	**krui**-du
seat (chair)	stoel, de	stool
(on bus, train, etc)	zitplaats, de	**zit**-plahts
seatbelt	veiligheidsgordel, de	**vei**-liCH-heits-**CHor**-del
second class	tweede klas	**tway**-du klas
second-hand	tweedehands	**tway**-du-hants
to see	zien	zeen
to sell	verkopen	ver-**koh**-pu
do you sell...?	verkoop je...?	ver-**kohp** yu...?
to send	zenden	**zen**-du
senior citizen	65-plusser	veif-en-zes-tiCH-**plues**-ser
serious	serieus	say-ree-**eus**
(illness)	ernstig	**ern**-stiCH
service charge	servicetoeslag, de	**ser**-vis-**too**-slaCH
is service included?	is de service inbegrepen?	is du **ser**-vis **in**-bu-CHray-pu?
service station	benzinestation, het	ben-**zee**-nu-sta-**shon**
set menu	dagmenu, het	**daCH**-mu-nuu
several	verschillende	ver-**sCHil**-lun-du
sex (gender)	sexe, de; geslacht	**sek**-su; CHu-**slaCHt**
(intercourse)	seks, de	seks
shade	schaduw, de	**sCHah**-doow

English	Dutch	Pronunciation
shallow	ondiep	**on**-deep
shampoo	shampoo, de	**sham**-poh
to share	delen	**day**-lu
sharp (razor, knife)	scherp	sCHerp
to shave	scheren	**sCHayr**-ru
she	zij	zei
sheet (for bed)	laken, het	**lah**-ku
shellfish	schelpdieren, de	**sCHelp**-deer-ru
sheltered	beschut	bu-**sCHuet**
to shine	schijnen	**sCHei**-nu
shirt	overhemd, het	**oh**-ver-hemt
shoe	schoen, de	sCHoon
shop	winkel, de	**wing**-kel
to shop	winkelen	**wing**-ku-lu
(for groceries)	boodschappen doen	**bohd**-sCHap-pu doon
shop assistant	verkoper, de	ver-**koh**-per
short	kort	kort
shorts	korte broek, de	**kor**-tu brook
shoulder	schouder, de	**sCHow**-der
to shout	roepen	**roo**-pu
show	show, de	show
to show	laten zien	**lah**-tu zeen
shower	douche, de	doosh
(rain)	bui, de	bui
to have a shower	douchen	**doo**-shu
to shrink	krimpen	**krim**-pu
shut (closed)	gesloten	CHu-**sloh**-tu
to shut	sluiten	**slui**-tu
sick (ill)	ziek	zeek
side	zijde, de	**zei**-du
to sightsee	zienswaardigheden bezoeken	**zeens**-wahr-diCH-**hay**-du bu-**zoo**-ku
sign (road, notice, etc)	bord, het	bort
to sign	tekenen	**tay**-ku-nu
signature	handtekening, de	**hant**-tay-ku-ning
silk	zijde, de	**zei**-du
silver	zilver	**zil**-ver

similar:	net als	net als
similar to		
since (time)	sinds	sints
(because)	omdat	**om**-dat
to sing	zingen	**zing**-u
single (not married)	ongetrouwd	**on**-CHu-trowt
(not double)	eenpersoons-	**ayn**-per-sohns
(ticket)	enkeltje, het	**eng**-kul-chu
sir	meneer	mu-**nayr**
sister	zus, de	zues
to sit	zitten	**zit**-tu
please, sit down	ga alsjeblieft zitten	CHah als-yu-**bleeft zit**-tu
size (clothes, shoes)	maat, de	maht
to skate	schaatsen	**sCHaht**-su
skates (ice)	schaatsen, de	**sCHaht**-su
(roller)	rolschaatsen, de	**rol**-sCHaht-su
skating rink	ijsbaan, de	**eis**-bahn
skin	huid, de	huit
skirt	rok, de	rok
sky	hemel, de	**hay**-mul
to sleep	slapen	**slah**-pu
to sleep in	uitslapen	**uit**-slah-pu
slice	snee, de	snay
slow(ly)	langzaam	**lang**-zahm
small	klein	klein
smell	reuk, de	reuk
to smell (of)	ruiken (naar)	**rui**-ku nahr
smile	glimlach, de	**CHlim**-laCH
to smile	glimlachen	**CHlim**-laCH-u
smoke	rook, de	rohk
to smoke	roken	**roh**-ku
I don't smoke	ik rook niet	ik rohk neet
may I smoke?	mag ik roken?	maCH ik **roh**-ku?
snack	snack, de	snek
to sneeze	niezen	**nee**-zu
snow	sneeuw, de	**snay**-oo
to snow	sneeuwen	**snay**-wu
it's snowing	het sneeuwt	ut **snay**-oot
so	zo	zoh

English	Dutch	Pronunciation
so much	zoveel	**zoh**-vayl
soap	zeep, de	zayp
sober	nuchter	**nueCH**-ter
sofa	bank, de	bank
soft	zacht	zaCHt
soft drink	frisdrank, de	**fris**-drank
soluble	oplosbaar	op-**los**-bahr
some (a few)	enkele	**eng**-ku-lu
someone	iemand	**ee**-mant
something	iets	eets
sometimes	soms	soms
somewhere	ergens	**er**-CHuns
son	zoon, de	zohn
song	lied, het	leet
soon	spoedig	**spoo**-diCH
as soon as possible	zo spoedig mogelijk	zoh **spoo**-diCH **moh**-CHu-luk
sore throat	keelpijn, de	**kayl**-pein
sorry: ***I'm sorry!***	het spijt me!	ut speit mu!
soup	soep, de	soop
sour	zuur	zuur
south	zuid	zuit
souvenir	souvenir, het	soo-vu-**neer**
sparkling	sprankelend	**sprang**-ku-lunt
to speak	spreken	**spray**-ku
do you speak English?	spreek je Engels?	sprayk yu **eng**-uls?
I don't speak Dutch	ik spreek geen Nederlands	ik sprayk CHayn **nay**-der-lants
special	speciaal	spay-see-**ahl**
speciality	specialiteit, de	spay-see-ah-lee-**teit**
speed	snelheid, de	**snel**-heit
speed limit	snelheidslimiet, de	**snel**-heits-lee-**meet**
to spell	spellen	**spel**-lu
how do you spell it?	hoe spel je het?	hoo spel yu ut?
to spend (money)	uitgeven	**uit**-CHay-vu
spices	specerijen, de	spay-su-**rei**-yu

English	Dutch	Pronunciation
spicy	pikant	pee-**kant**
spinach	spinazie, de	spee-**nah**-zee
spirits	sterke dranken, de	**ster**-ku **drang**-ku
spoon	lepel, de	**lay**-pel
spot (place)	plek, de	plek
spring (season)	lente, de	**len**-tu
square (in town)	plein, het	plein
stadium	stadion, het	**stah**-dee-on
staff	personeel, het	per-soh-**nayl**
stain	vlek, de	vlek
stairs	trap, de	trap
stamp (postage)	postzegel, de	**post**-zay-CHul
to stand	staan	stahn
to start	starten	**star**-tu
starter (meal)	voorgerecht, het	**vohr**-CHu-reCHt
station	station, het	sta-**shon**
statue	standbeeld, het	**stant**-baylt
stay	verblijf, het	ver-**bleif**
enjoy your stay!	een plezierig verblijf!	un plu-**zee**-riCH ver-**bleif**!

English	Dutch	Pronunciation
to stay	blijven	**blei**-vu
I'm staying at a hotel	ik logeer in een hotel	ik loh-**shayr** in un hoh-**tel**
steak	biefstuk, de	**beef**-stuk
to steal	stelen	**stay**-lu
steep	stijl	steil
is it steep?	is het stijl?	is ut steil?
stereo	stereo, de	**stay**-ray-oh
sterling (pounds)	Britse ponden, de	**brit**-su **pon**-du
to stick (with glue)	lijmen	**lei**-mu
sticking plaster	pleister, de	**pleis**-ter
still (not moving)	stil	stil
(not sparkling)	zonder prik	**zon**-der prik
(yet)	nog	noCH
stolen	gestolen	CHu-**stoh**-lu
stomach	maag, de	mahCH
stomach upset	maagstoring, de	**mahCH**-stoh-ring

English	Dutch	Pronunciation
stone	steen, de	stayn
to stop (come to a halt)	stoppen	**stop**-pu
(stop doing something)	stoppen met...	**stop**-pu met...
store (shop)	winkel, de	**wing**-kel
storey	verdieping, de	ver-**dee**-ping
storm	storm, de	storm
story	verhaal, het	ver-**hahl**
straightaway	direct	dee-**rect**
straight on	rechtdoor	**reCHt**-dohr
strange	vreemd	vraymt
strawberry	aardbei, de	**ahrd**-bei
street	straat, de	straht
street map	stratenplan, het	**strah**-tun-plan
strength	sterkte	**sterk**-tu
stroke (medical)	beroerte, de	bu-**roor**-tu
strong	sterk	sterk
strong coffee	sterke koffie	**ster**-ku **kof**-fee
strong tea	sterke thee	**ster**-ku tay
student	student, de	stuu-**dent**
student discount	studentenkorting, de	stuu-**den**-tun-**kor**-ting
stung (by insect)	gebeten	CHu-**bay**-tu
stupid	dom	dom
suddenly	plotseling	**plot**-su-ling
suede	suede, het	suu-**eh**-du
sugar	suiker, de	**sui**-ker
icing sugar	poedersuiker, de	**poo**-der-sui-ker
sugar-free	suikervrij	sui-ker-**vrei**
to suggest	voorstellen	**vohr**-stel-lu
suit	kostuum, het	kos-**tuum**
suitcase	koffer, de	**kof**-fer
sum (of money)	som, de	som
summer	zomer, de	**zoh**-mer
sun	zon, de	zon
to sunbathe	zonnebaden	**zon**-nu-bah-du
sunburn	zonnebrand, de	**zon**-nu-brant
Sunday	zondag	**zon**-daCH
sunglasses	zonnebril, de	**zon**-nu-bril
sunny	zonnig	**zon**-niCH
it's sunny	het is zonnig	ut is **zon**-niCH

English	Dutch	Pronunciation
sunrise	zonsopgang, de	**zons**-op-CHang
sunset	zonsondergang, de	**zons**-on-der-CHang
sunstroke	zonnesteek, de	**zon**-nu-stayk
suntan	kleur, de	kleur
suntan lotion	zonnebrand-lotion, de	**zon**-nu-brant-loht-**shohn**
supermarket	supermarkt, de	**suu**-per-markt
supper	avondmaal, het	**ah**-vont-mahl
supplement	supplement, het	suep-plu-**ment**
to supply	voorzien	**vohr**-zeen
surcharge	toeslag, de	**too**-slaCH
sure	zeker	**zay**-ker
I'm sure	ik weet het zeker	ik wayt ut **zay**-ker
surname	achternaam, de	**aCH**-ter-nahm
my surname is...	mijn achternaam is...	mein **aCH**-ter-nahm is...
surprise	verrassing, de	ver-**ras**-sing
to sweat	zweten	**zway**-tu
sweet (not savoury)	zoet	zoot
sweetener	zoetstof, de	**zoot**-stof
sweets	snoepjes, de	**snoop**-yus
to swell	opzwellen	**op**-zwel-lu
to swim	zwemmen	**zwem**-mu
swimming pool	zwembad, het	**zwem**-bat
swimsuit	zwempak, het	**zwem**-pak
to switch off	uitdoen	**uit**-doon
to switch on	aandoen	**ahn**-doon
swollen	opgezwollen	**op**-CHu-zwol-lu
syringe	injectienaald, de	in-**yek**-tsee-nahlt

T

English	Dutch	Pronunciation
table	tafel, de	**tah**-fel
tablet	pil, de	pil
table wine	tafelwijn, de	**tah**-fel-wein
to take (carry)	meenemen	**may**-nay-mu
(to grab, seize)	pakken	**pak**-ku
(medicine, etc)	nemen	**nay**-mu
how long does it take?	hoe lang duurt het?	hoo lang duurt ut?

English	Dutch	Pronunciation
take-away (food)	afhaal-	**af**-hahl
to take off	uitdoen	**uit**-doon
to talk to	praten met	**prah**-tu met
tall	groot	CHroht
tangerine	mandarijn, de	man-dah-**rein**
tap water	kraanwater, het	**krahn**-wah-ter
tart	taart, de	tahrt
taste	smaak, de	smahk
to taste	proeven	**proo**-vu
can I taste it?	mag ik het proeven?	maCH ik ut **proo**-vu?
tax	belasting, de	bu-**las**-ting
taxi	taxi, de	**tak**-see
tea	thee, de	tay
lemon tea	citroenthee, de	see-**troon**-tay
strong tea with milk	sterke thee met melk, de	**ster**-ku tay met melk
to teach	leren	**layr**-ru
teacher	docent, de	doh-**sent**
team	team, het	team
teaspoon	theelepel, de	**tay**-lay-pel
teeth	tanden, de	**tan**-du
telephone	telefoon, de	**tay**-lu-fohn
mobile telephone	mobiele telefoon, de; gsm, de	moh-**bee**-lu **tay**-lu-fohn; **CHay**-es-em
to telephone	opbellen	**op**-bel-lu
telephone box	telefooncel, de	**tay**-lu-fohn-sell
telephone call	telefoongesprek, het	**tay**-lu-fohn-CHu-**sprek**
telephone card	telefoonkaart, de	**tay**-lu-fohn-kahrt
telephone number	telefoonnummer, het	**tay**-lu-fohn-**nuem**-mer
to tell	vertellen	ver-**tel**-lu
temperature	temperatuur, de	tem-pu-rah-**tuur**
I have a temperature	ik heb koorts	ik heb kohrts
temporary	tijdelijk	**tei**-du-luk
to test (try out)	testen	**tes**-tu
to text (phone)	sms-en	es-em-es-u

than	dan	dan
to thank	bedanken	bu-**dang**-ku
thank you/ thanks	dank je	dank yu
thank you very much	dankjewel	dank -yu-**wel**
that (de- words)	die	dee
(het- words)	dat	dat
that one		
(de- words)	die	dee
(het- words)	dat	dat
the	de; het	du; ut
theatre	theater, het	tay-**ah**-ter
theft	diefstal, de	**deef**-stal
their	hun	huen
them	hen	hen
then	toen	toon
there	daar	dahr
there is	er is	er is
there are	er zijn	er zein
these; those	deze; die	**day**-zu; dee
they	zij	zei
thick	dik	dik
thief	dief, de	deef
thin	dun	duen
thing	ding, het	ding
to think	denken	**deng**-ku
(opinion)	vinden	**vin**-du
to be thirsty	dorst hebben	dorst **heb**-bu
I'm thirsty	ik heb dorst	ik heb dorst
this (de- words)	deze	**day**-zu
(het- words)	dit	dit
throat	keel, de	kayl
through	door	dohr
to throw away	weggooien	**weCH**-CHoy-yu
thunder storm	onweersbui, de	**on**-wayrs-bui
Thursday	donderdag	**don**-der-daCH
ticket	kaartje, het	**kahr**-chu
single ticket	enkeltje, het	**eng**-kel-chu
return ticket	retourtje, het	ru-**toor**-chu
ticket office	kassa, de	**kas**-sah
tidy	netjes	**net**-chus

to tidy up	opruimen	**op**-rui-mu
tie	stropdas, de	**strop**-das
tight	strak	strak
tights	panty, de	**pan**-tee
till (until)	tot	tot
time	tijd, de	teit
what time is it?	hoe laat is het?	hoo laht is ut?
do you have the time?	weet u hoe laat het is?	wayt uu hoo laht ut is?
timetable (train)	dienstregeling, de	**deenst**-ray-CHu-ling
tin (can)	blik, het	blik
tin-opener	blikopener, de	**blik**-oh-pen-er
to tip	fooi geven	**foh**-ee **CHay**-vu
tired	moe	moo
tissues	zakdoekjes, de	**zak**-dook-yus
to	naar	nahr
to the airport	naar het vliegveld	nahr ut **vleeCH**-velt
toast (to eat)	geroosterd brood, het	CHu-**roh**-stert broht
(raising glass)	toost, de	tohst
tobacco	tabak, de	tah-**bak**
tobacconist	sigarenwinkel, de	see-**CHar**-ru-wing-kel
today	vandaag	van-**dahCH**
together	samen	**sah**-mu
toilet	toilet, het; WC, de	twa-**let**; way-**say**
tomato	tomaat, de;	toh-**maht**
tomorrow	morgen	**mor**-CHu
tomorrow morning	morgenochtend	mor-CHun-**oCH**-tunt
tongue	tong, de	tong
tonight	vannacht	van-**naCHt**
tonsillitis	amandelontsteking, de	ah-**man**-del-ont-**stay**-king
too	te	tu
(also)	ook	ohk
too big	te groot	tu CHroht

English	Dutch	Pronunciation
too small	te klein	tu klein
too noisy	te lawaaierig	tu lah-**wah**-yu-riCH
tooth	tand, de	tant
toothache	kiespijn, de	**kees**-pein
toothbrush	tandenborstel, de	**tan**-du-bor-stel
toothpaste	tandpasta, de	**tant**-pas-tah
total (amount)	totaal, het	toh-**tahl**
to touch	aanraken	**ahn**-rah-ku
tough (meat)	taai	**tah**-ee
tour (trip)	tour, de	toor
guided tour	rondleiding met gids	**ront**-lei-ding met CHits
tourist	toerist, de	too-**rist**
tourist information	VVV; toeristische informatie, de	vay-vay-vay; too-**ris**-tee-su in-for-**mah**-tsee
towel	handdoek, de	**hant**-dook
tower	toren, de	**toh**-ru
town	stad, de	stat
town centre	centrum, het	**sen**-truem
town hall	stadhuis, het	**stat**-huis
town plan	plattegrond, de	**plat**-tu-CHront
toxic	vergiftig	ver-**CHif**-tiCH
toy	speelgoed, het	**spayl**-CHoot
toy shop	speelgoedwinkel, de	**spayl**-CHoot-**wing**-kel
traditional	traditioneel	trah-dee-tsee-oh-**nayl**
traffic	verkeer, het	ver-**kayr**
traffic jam	file, de	**fee**-lu
traffic lights	verkeerslichten, de	ver-**kayrs**-liCH-tu
train	trein, de	trein
the first/next/last train	de eerste/volgende/laatste trein	du **ayr**-stu/**vol**-CHun-du/**laht**-stu trein
tram	tram, de	tram
tranquillizer	kalmerend middel, het	kal-**mayr**-runt **mid**-del
to transfer (money)	overmaken	**oh**-ver-mah-ku

English	Dutch	Pronunciation
to translate	vertalen	ver-**tah**-lu
to travel	reizen	**rei**-zu
travel agent	reisagentschap, het	**reis**-ah-CHent-sCHap
trip	reis, de	reis
trolley	wagentje, het	**wah**-CHun-chu
trouble	moeilijkheden, de	**moo**-ee-luk-hay-du
trousers	broek, de	brook
true	waar	wahr
to try (attempt)	proberen	proh-**bayr**-ru
to try on (clothes, shoes)	passen	**pas**-su
Tuesday	dinsdag	**dins**-daCH
tulip	tulp, de	tuelp
to turn	draaien	**drah**-yu
to turn around	omdraaien	**om**-drah-yu
to turn off (light, engine, etc)	uitdoen	**uit**-doon
(tap)	dichtdraaien	**diCHt**-drah-yu
to turn on (light, etc)	aandoen	**ahn**-doon
(tap)	opendraaien	**oh**-pen-drah-yu
tweezers	pincet, het	pin-**set**
twice	tweemaal	**tway**-mahl
typical	typisch	**tee**-pees
U		
ugly	lelijk	**lay**-luk
umbrella	paraplu, de	pah-rah-**pluu**
uncle	oom, de	ohm
uncomfortable	ongemakkelijk	on-CHu-**mak**-ku-luk
unconscious	bewusteloos	bu-**wues**-tu-lohs
under	onder	**on**-der
underground (metro)	metro, de	**may**-troh
underpants	onderbroek, de	**on**-der-brook
to understand (knowledge)	begrijpen	bu-**CHrei**-pu
(hear)	verstaan	ver-**stahn**

English	Dutch	Pronunciation
underwear	ondergoed, het	**on**-der-CHoot
to undress	uitkleden	**uit**-klay-du
unemployed	werkloos	**werk**-lohs
unhappy	ontevreden	on-tu-**vray**-du
to be unhappy with...	ontevreden zijn met...	on-tu-**vray**-du zein met...
United Kingdom	Verenigd Koninkrijk, het	ver-**ay**-niCHt **koh**-ning-kreik
United States	Verenigde Staten, de	ver-**ay**-niCH-du **stah**-tu
university	universiteit, de	uu-nee-ver-see-**teit**
unlikely	onwaarschijnlijk	on-wahr-**sCHein**-luk
to unlock	openmaken	**oh**-pen-mah-ku
to unpack (suitcases)	uitpakken	**uit**-pak-ku
unpleasant	onplezierig	on-plu-**zeer**-riCH
until	tot	tot
unusual	ongewoon	**on**-CHu-wohn
up	op	op
to get up	opstaan	**op**-stahn
urgent	dringend	**dring**-unt
us	ons	ons
USA	VS	vay-**es**
to use	gebruiken	CHu-**brui**-ku
useful	nuttig	**nuet**-tiCH
usual	gebruikelijk	CHu-**brui**-ku-luk
usually	gewoonlijk	CHu-**wohn**-luk

V

English	Dutch	Pronunciation
vacancies (hotel)	kamers vrij	**kah**-mers vrei
vacant	vrij	vrei
vacation	vakantie, de	va-**kan**-see
valid	geldig	**CHel**-diCH
valuable	waardevol	**wahr**-du-vol
valuables	waardevolle zaken	**wahr**-du-vol-lu **zah**-ku
value	waarde	**wahr**-du
VAT	BTW	bay-tay-way
veal	kalfsvlees, het	**kalfs**-vlays

English	Dutch	Pronunciation
vegan	veganist, de	vay-CHah-**nist**
I'm vegan	ik ben veganist	ik ben vay-CHah-**nist**
vegetables	groente, de	**CHroon**-tu
vegetarian	vegetariër, de	vay-CHu-**tah**-ree-yer
I'm vegetarian	ik ben vegetariër	ik ben vay-CHu-**tah**-ree-yer
vending machine	automaat, de	ow-toh-**maht**
very	zeer	zayr
video camera	videocamera, de	**vee**-day-oh-**kah**-mu-rah
video cassette	videocassette, de	**vee**-day-oh-cas-**set**-tu
view	uitzicht, het	**uit**-ziCHt
village	dorp, het	dorp
vinegar	azijn, de	ah-**zein**
virus	virus, het	**vee**-rue
visa	visum, het	**vee**-suem
visit	bezoek, het	bu-**zook**
to visit	bezoeken	bu-**zoo**-ku
visitor	bezoeker, de	bu-**zoo**-ker
voice	stem, de	stem
to vomit	overgeven	**oh**-ver-CHay-vu
voucher	bon, de	bon

W

English	Dutch	Pronunciation
to wait for	wachten op	**waCH**-tu op
waiter	ober, de; kelner, de	**oh**-ber; **kel**-ner
waiting room	wachtkamer, de	**waCHt**-kah-mer
to wake up	wakker worden	**wak**-ker **wor**-du
to walk	lopen	**loh**-pu
(leisure)	wandelen	**wan**-du-lu
walk	wandeling, de	**wan**-du-ling
wall	muur, de	muur
wallet	portefeuille, de	por-tu-**feu**-yu
to want	willen	**wil**-lu
I want...	ik wil...	ik wil...
we want...	wij willen...	wei **wil**-lu...

warning triangle	gevarendriehoek, de	CHu-**vah**-run-dree-hook
to wash	wassen	**was**-su
wasp	wesp, de	wesp
watch	horloge, het	hor-**loh**-shu
to watch	kijken	**kei**-ku
water	water, het	**wah**-ter
mineral water	mineraal water, het	mee-nu-**rahl**-wah-ter
still water	water zonder prik, het	**wah**-ter **zon**-der prik
waves	golven, de	**CHol**-vu
way in (entrance)	ingang, de	**in**-CHang
way out (exit)	uitgang, de	**uit**-CHang
we	wij; we	wei; wu
weak	zwak	zwak
weather	weer, het	wayr
weather forecast	weersverwachting, de	**wayrs**-ver-waCH-ting
wedding	huwelijk, het	**huu**-wu-luk
Wednesday	woensdag	**woons**-daCH
week	week, de	wayk
this/last/next week	deze/vorige/volgende week	**day**-zu/**vor**-ri-CHu/**vol**-CHun-du wayk
weekday	werkdag	**werk**-daCH
weekend	weekend, het	**wee**-kent
this/next weekend	dit/volgend weekend	dit/**vol**-CHunt **wee**-kent
weekly	wekelijks	**way**-ku-luks
to weigh	wegen	**way**-CHu
weight	gewicht, het	CHu-**wiCHt**
welcome	welkom	**wel**-kom
well	goed	CHoot
well-done (steak)	doorbakken	dohr-**bak**-ku
Welsh	Welsh	welsh
wet	nat	nat
what	wat	wat
what is it?	wat is er?	wat is er?
when?	wanneer?	wan-**nayr**?
where?	waar?	wahr?

English	Dutch	Pronunciation
which?	welke?	**wel**-ku?
while	terwijl	ter-**weil**
whipped cream	slagroom, de	**slaCH**-rohm
white	wit	wit
who?	wie?	wee?
whole	heel	hayl
wholemeal bread	volkorenbrood, het	vol-**koh**-run-broht
whose	van wie	van wee
whose is it?	van wie is het?	van wee is ut?
why?	waarom?	wah-**rom**?
wide	breed	brayt
width	breedte, de	**brayt**-tu
wife	echtgenote, de	**eCHt**-CHu-noh-tu
to win	winnen	**win**-nu
wind	wind, de	wint
it's windy	het waait	ut **wah**-eet
windmill	windmolen, de	**wint**-moh-lu
window	raam, het	rahm
(shop)	etalage, de	ay-tah-**lah**-shu
windscreen	voorruit, de	**vohr**-ruit
wine	wijn, de	wein
red/white/rosé wine	rode/witte/rosé wijn, de	**roh**-du/**wit**-tu/roh-**say** wein
sweet/dry wine	zoete/droge wijn, de	**zoo**-tu/**droh**-CHu wein
winter	winter, de	**win**-ter
with	met	met
with ice/milk/sugar	met ijs/melk/suiker	met eis/melk/**sui**-ker
without	zonder	**zon**-der
without ice/milk/sugar	zonder ijs/melk/suiker	**zon**-der eis/melk/**sui**-ker
woman	vrouw, de	vrow
wonderful	schitterend	**sCHit**-tu-runt
woods	bossen, de	**bos**-su
word	woord, het	wohrt
to work (person, machine)	werken	**wer**-ku
it doesn't work	hij doet het niet	hei doot ut neet

world wereld, de **wayr**-ult
worried bezorgd bu-**zorCHt**
worse slechter **sleCH**-ter
to wrap up inpakken **in**-pak-ku
to write schrijven **sCHrei**-vu
please write it down schrijf het op, alstublieft sCHreif ut op, als-tuu-**bleeft**
wrong verkeerd ver-**kayrt**
what's wrong? wat is er? wat is er?

X

x-ray röntgenfoto, de **reunt**-CHun-foh-toh

Y

year jaar, het yahr
this/last/next year dit/vorig/volgend jaar dit/ **vor**-riCH/**vol**-CHunt yahr
yearly jaarlijks **yahr**-luks
yellow geel CHayl
Yellow Pages® Gouden Gids, de **CHow**-du CHits
yes ja yah
yesterday gisteren **CHis**-tu-ru
yet nog noCH
not yet nog niet noCH neet
yoghurt yoghurt, de **yoh**-Choort
you (singular) je ye
(plural) jullie **yuel**-lee
(formal) u uu
young jong yong
your (singular) jouw yow
(plural) jullie **yuel**-lee
(formal) uw uuw

Z

zero nul nuel
zone zone, de **zoh**-nu
zoo dierentuin, de **deer**-un-tuin

Dutch - English

A

aan on *(light, TV)*
aanbevelen to recommend
aangeven to declare
aangenaam kennis te maken pleased to meet you
aankomen to arrive
aankomst, de arrival
aanraken to touch
niet aanraken do not touch
aansteker, de lighter *(cigarette)*
aantrekkelijk attractive
aardappel, de potato
aardig kind; nice
accommodatie, de accommodation
achter behind
achternaam, de surname
ademen to breathe
adviseren, to advise
afstand, de distance
airconditioning, de air-conditioning
al already
alcoholisch alcoholic
alcoholvrij non-alcoholic
alle all; every
alleen alone
allergisch voor allergic to
alles everything
als when; if; as; like
alsjeblieft please *(informal)*
alstublieft please *(formal)*
altijd always
ambassade, de embassy
ambulance, de ambulance
Amerika America
Amerikaans American
ander other
de andere the other one
anders niets nothing else
anders nog iets? anything else?
annuleren to cancel
antwoord, het answer
apart separate
apotheek, de dispensing chemist *(pharmacist)*
arm, de arm
arts, de doctor
asbak, de ashtray
astma, de asthma
a.u.b. please *(abbreviation)*
Australië Australia
Australisch Australian
auto, de car

autoweg, de motorway
autopech, de car breakdown
autoveerboot, de car ferry
autoweg, de motorway
avond, de evening
's avonds in the evening
avondeten, het evening meal

B

baas, de boss
baby, de baby
badkamer, de bathroom
bagage, de luggage
bakker, de baker
balie, de (check-in) desk
band, de tyre
bang frightened
bank, de bank
bed, het bed
bediening, de service *(in restaurant)*
beeld, het sculpture; statue
been, het bone; leg
beet, de bite; sting
beetje: ***een beetje*** a bit; a little
begane grond, de ground floor
beginnen to begin
beha, de bra
behalve except
bellen to ring
beneden down; below
bent u in orde? are you all right?
benzinestation, het petrol station
beroemd famous
beroven to rob
beste best; *(letter)* dear
bestellen to order
bestelling, de order
betaald paid
betalen to pay
betaling, de payment
betekenen to mean
beter better
bevatten to contain
bevestigen to confirm
bewegen to move
bewolkt cloudy
bewusteloos unconscious
bezet occupied *(toilet)*
bezoeken to visit
bezorgd worried
bibliotheek, de library
bier, het beer; lager
bij at; near
bijna almost
bijvoorbeeld for example
binnen indoors

Dutch - English

binnenband, de inner tube
bnnenkomen to enter
bioscoop, de cinema
blaar, de blister
bladzijde, de page
bleek pale
blijven to remain; to stay
blik, het can; tin
blikopener, de tin-opener
blindedarmontsteking, de appendicitis
bloed, het blood
bloem, de flower; flour
bloembol, de bulb
bloembollenvelden, de bulb fields
boeken to book
boerderij, de farm
boete, de fine *(to be paid)*
bollenveld, het bulb field
boodschap, de message
boodschappen, de shopping
boom, de tree
boos angry
boottocht, de boat trip
bord, het dish; plate; sign
borst, de breast
bos, het wood *(forest)*
boven above; upstairs; over
braden to roast
brand fire
brandblusser, de fire extinguisher
brandstof, de fuel
breekbaar breakable
breken to break
brengen to bring; to fetch
breuk, de fracture
brief, de letter
briefje, het note; bank note
briefkaart, de postcard
brievenbus, de letterbox
bril, de spectacles
Brits British
Britse pond, het pound sterling
broek, de trousers
broer, de brother
brood, het bread; loaf
broodje, het bun; bread roll
BTW VAT
buiten outside; outdoor
buik, de stomach
buitenlands foreign
bus, de bus; coach
bushalte, de bus stop
bustocht, de bus tour; coach trip

C

cadeau, het gift; present
cadeauwinkel, de gift shop
café, het café *(bar)*
cafetaria, de snack bar
camcorder, de camcorder
camera, de camera
camping, de campsite
Canada Canada
Canadees Canadian
Carnaval Carnival *(4 days preceding Lent)*
cent euro cent *(1 euro = 100 euro cents)*
centrum, het centre; town centre
cheque, de cheque
Cola Coke®, cola
coffeeshop, de coffee shop
conferentie, de conference
consulaat, het consulate
contactlenzen, de contact lenses
contant cash
controleren to check
coupé, de compartment *(in train)*
couvert, het cover charge
creditcard, de credit card
crème, de cream *(lotion)*
crèmespoeling, de conditioner

D

daar there
daarna afterwards
daarom therefore
dag, de day
dag! goodbye!; hello!
dagelijks daily
dagmenu, het set menu
dames ladies *(toilet)*
dan than
dank je/u thank you *(informal/formal)*
dank je/u wel thank you very much *(informal/formal)*
dat that
datum, de date
de the
de heer (dhr) Mr
deel, het part
defect out of order
delen to share
denken to think
deur, de door
deuren sluiten close the doors *(sign)*

Dutch – English

deze	this; these
deze keer	this time
dezelfde	same
dicht	shut; closed
die	that; those
dieet, het	diet
dienstregeling, de	timetable
diep	deep
dier, het	animal
dierentuin, de	zoo
dik	thick
diner, het	dinner
dineren	to have dinner
ding, het	thing
direct	at once
dit	this
dochter, de	daughter
document, het	document
doen	to do
dokter, de	doctor
dom	stupid
donder, de	thunder
donker	dark
dood	dead
door	through
dorp, het	village
dorst, de	thirst
douane, de	customs
douche, de	shower
dragen	to carry; to wear
drank, de	drink
dringend	urgent
drinken	to drink
drinkwater, het	drinking water
drogen	to dry
drogist, de	chemist
dronken	drunk
droog	dry
drop, de	liquorice
druk	busy; crowded
dubbel	double
Duits	German
Duitsland	Germany
duizelig	dizzy
dun	thin
duur	expensive
duwen	to push; push *(sign)*

E

eb, de	low tide
echt	genuine; real
een	a
één	one
eend, de	duck
éénpersoonsbed, het	single bed
éénpersoonskamer, de	single room
éénrichtingsverkeer	one-way traffic

eens	once
eerste hulp, de	first aid
eerste klas, de	first class
eerste verdieping, de	first floor
eetkamer, de	dining room
eeuw, de	century
EHBO	first-aid post *(sign)*
ei, het	egg
eieren, de	eggs
eindigen	to finish; to end
eindpunt, het	terminus
elektrisch	electric
en	and
Engeland	England
Engels	English
enig	only
enige	some
enkel	single
enkele	a few
enkele reis, de	single *(journey)*
er	there
er is een misverstand	there's been a misunderstanding
er is/er zijn	there is/there are
ernstig	serious *(accident, etc)*
etalage, de	shop window
eten	to eat
Europa	Europe
Europees	European

F

faciliteiten, de	facilities
factuur, de	invoice
familie, de	family
feest, het	party
fiets, de	bicycle
fietsen	to cycle
fietspad, het	cycle path
fietstocht, de	cycle tour
fietsverhuur	cycle hire
file, de	traffic jam
filet	fillet
film, de	film
flat, de	flat *(apartment)*
flauwgevallen	fainted
fles, de	bottle
fooi, de	tip *(to waiter, etc)*
foto, de	photograph
fotograferen	to photograph
fotokopie, de	photocopy
fout, de	mistake
fout	wrong *(incorrect)*
Frankrijk	France
Frans	French
frites; friet	french fries

fritessaus mayonnaise for french fries
frituur snack bar; chip shop
fruit, het fruit

G

gaan to go
ga linksaf turn left
ga rechtsaf turn right
galerie, de art gallery
gang, de course *(of meal)*; aisle
garage, de garage
gast, de guest
gebak, het cake
gebakken fried
gebakken ei, het fried egg
gebeuren to happen
geboortedatum, de date of birth
gebouw, het building
gebroken broken
gebruiken to use
gedurende during
geel yellow
geen none; not any
geen ingang no entry *(sign)*
geen uitgang no exit *(sign)*
gegrild grilled
gehandicapt handicapped
gek mad
gekookt boiled
gekookt ei, het boiled egg
geld, het cash; money
geld inwerpen insert coins *(sign)*
geld terug change
geldig valid
geloven to believe
gelukkig happy; fortunately
gemakkelijk easy
geneesmiddel, het drug *(medicinal)*
genieten to enjoy
genoeg enough
gepensioneerde, de pensioner
gereserveerd reserved
gescheiden divorced
gesloten closed; shut
getrouwd married
gevaar danger *(sign)*
gevaarlijk dangerous
gevarendriehoek, de warning triangle *(car)*
geven to give
gevonden voorwerpen lost property *(sign)*
gewend aan used to

ik ben gewend aan... I'm used to...
gewond injured
gewoon usual
gezwollen swollen
gids, de guide
giftig poisonous
gisteren yesterday
glas, het glass
goed good; all right; well
goedemiddag good afternoon
goedemorgen good morning
goedkoop cheap
golven, de waves
gracht, de canal *(in town)*
grap, de joke
gratis free
grens, de border
griep, de flu
groente, de vegetables
groot big; large; tall; great
Groot Brittannië Great Britain
grot, de cave
groter bigger

H

haar her
haar, het hair
haast hurry
ik heb haast I'm in a hurry
halen to fetch; to bring; to get
halfvolle melk, de semi-skimmed milk
hallo hello
handbagage, de hand luggage
handtekening, de signature
hard hard; loud; fast
hartelijk gefeliciteerd! congratulations!
hartig savoury
haven, de harbour; port
hebben to have
heel whole; quite
heet hot
help! help!
heren gents *(toilets)*
herfst, de autumn
herhalen to repeat
herinneren to remember
herkennen to recognize
het the; it
hetzelfde the same
heuvel, de hill
hier here
hij he
hoe how *(in what way)*

hoek, de corner
hoeveel? how much?; how many?
hoi hi *(informal greeting)*
Holland Holland
hond, de dog
hondsdolheid, de rabies
hongerig hungry
hoofdgerecht, het main course
hoofdpijn, de headache
hoofdstad, de capital
hoog high
hooikoorts, de hay fever
hopen to hope
horen to hear
hotel, het hotel
houden to hold; to keep
houden van to like; to love
huis, het house; home
huren to hire; to rent
huwelijk, het wedding

I

ieder any; each; every
iedereen everyone
iemand someone
Ierland Ireland
Iers Irish
iets something
ijs, het ice; ice cream
roomijs dairy ice cream
waterijsje ice lolly
ijssalon, de ice cream parlour
ik I
in in; inside; into; over
in plaats van instead of
inclusief included
informatie, de information
ingang, de entrance; way in
inlichtingen enquiries
insectenbeet, de insect bite
instappen to get in *(vehicle)*
Intercity, de intercity train
intypen; intoetsen to key in
invalide disabled
invullen to fill in *(form)*
inwisselen to change *(money)*; to cash *(cheque)*
is is

J

ja yes
ja, alstublieft/graag yes, please

jaar, het	year
jas, de	coat
je; jij	you *(sing. informal)*
jenever, de	Dutch gin
jong	young
jongen, de	boy
joods	Jewish
journaal	news *(on TV)*
jullie	you *(plural informal)*

K

kaart, de	card; map; ticket
kaartverkoop, de	ticket sales; box office
kaas, de	cheese
kalfsvlees, het	veal
kalkoen, de	turkey
kamer, de	room
kan ik...?	can I...?; may I...?
kanaal, het	channel
kapel, de	chapel
kapot	broken
kapper, de	hairdresser
kassa, de	cash desk; till
kassabon, de	receipt
kathedraal, de	cathedral
katholiek	Catholic
kauwgom, de	chewing gum
keel, de	throat
kennen	to know; to be acquainted with
kerk, de	church
kermis, de	funfair
Kerstmis	Christmas
kg,	kilo
kiespijn, de	toothache
kijken (naar)	to watch; to look (at)
kind, het	child
kinderen, de	children
kip, de	chicken
klaar	ready; finished
klacht, de	complaint
klant, de	client; customer
kleedkamer, de	changing room
klein	little; small
kleren, de	clothes
kleur, de	colour
klok, de	clock; church bell
klompen, de	clogs
klooster, het	monastery
kloppen	to knock; knock *(sign)*
km	kilometre
knoflook, de	garlic
koekje, het	biscuit
koel	cool

Dutch – English

koers, de (exchange) rate
koffer, de case; suitcase
koffie, de coffee
koken to cook; to boil
komen to come
kom binnen! come in!
komkommer, de cucumber
koninklijk royal
kop, de cup; head *(of animal)*
kopen to buy
kopie, de copy
kort short; brief
korting, de reduction
kosten to cost
koud cold
kraan, de tap
krant, de newspaper
krijgen to get; to receive
kunnen to be able
kus, de kiss
kussen to kiss
kust, de coast; seaside
kustwacht, de coastguard

L

laag low; shallow
laat late
land, het country; nation; land
lang long; tall; large
langzaam slow; slowly
later later
leeftijd, de age
leeg empty
leiden to guide
lekker tasty; nice; pleasant
lenen to lend; to borrow
lente, de spring *(season)*
lepel, de spoon
leren to learn; to teach
leuk nice; funny *(amusing)*
leven to live
lezen to read
liefde, de love
liegen to lie
lieve dear
liften to hitchhike
liggen to lie down
links left
linksaf gaan turn left
liter litre
loket, het window *(ticket office)*; counter
loodvrije benzine, de unleaded petrol
lopen to walk
luchtpost, de air mail

lucifers, de matches
lui lazy
luid loud
luier, de nappy
luisteren to listen

M

maag, de stomach
maaltijd, de meal
maand, de month
maandverband, het sanitary towel
maar but
maat, de size
machine, de machine
mager skimmed *(milk, etc)*
maken to make *(generally)*
manier, de way *(manner)*
markt, de market
medicijn, het medicine
meer more
meer, het lake
meeste most
meisje, het girl
meisjesnaam, de maiden name
mejuffrouw Miss
melk, de milk
meneer Mr; Sir
mens, de human being
menstruatie, de period *(menstruation)*
menu, het menu
mes, het knife
met with
meter metre
metro, de underground *(metro)*
mevrouw (mevr.) Mrs, Ms.
middag, de afternoon
midden middle; medium
minder less
minst least
mis, de mass *(church)*
missen miss *(train, etc)*
mistig foggy
misverstand, het misunderstanding
modieus fashionable
moe tired
moeder, de mother
moeilijk difficult
mogelijk possible
molen, de mill; windmill
moment, het moment
mond, de mouth
mooi beautiful; fine; pretty
morgen tomorrow

Dutch – English

morning-after-pil emergency contraception
mousserend sparkling
mug, de mosquito
munt, de coin; mint *(herb)*
muntgeld, het coins
musea, de museums

N

na after
naakt naked; nude
naam, de name
naar to
naast beside
nacht, de night
nagel, de fingernail
nagerecht, het dessert
nat wet
natte verf wet paint
nationaliteit, de nationality
natuurreservaat, het nature reserve
Nederland The Netherlands
Nederlands Dutch
nee no
nemen to catch *(bus, etc)*; to take
netnummer, het dialling code
niemand nobody
niet not
niets nothing
nieuw new
Nieuwjaar New Year
nieuws, het news
nodig necessary
nog still; yet
noodgeval, het emergency
nooduitgang, de emergency exit
nooit never
noord north
nu now
nul zero
nummer, het number
nuttig useful

O

ober, de waiter
of or
ogenblik, het moment
omleiding, de diversion *(traffic)*
omweg, de detour
onder below; under
ondergoed, het underwear
ondertekenen to sign
ongeluk, het accident; crash; bad luck
ongelukkig unhappy
ongetrouwd unmarried
ongeveer approximately
onmiddellijk immediately

onmogelijk impossible
ons (onze) our
ons, het Dutch ounce; 100 g
ontbijt, het breakfast
ontmoeten to meet
ontsmetten to disinfect
ontsteking, de infection
ontwikkelen to develop
onweersbui, de thunderstorm
oog, het eye
ook also; too
oom, de uncle
oor, het ear
oorlog, de war
oost east
op up; on; above
opbellen to phone
open open
openbaar public
openen to open
oppas, de babysitter
oppassen to mind; to be careful
oranje orange *(colour)*
oud old
ouders, de parents
over in; over; about *(relating to)*
overmorgen the day after tomorrow
overtreding, de offence *(crime)*

P

p.a. care of; c/o
paard, het horse
pad, het path
pakken to take; to grab; to pack
pak maar take it
pakje, het packet; parcel
paleis, het palace
paling, de eel
pannenkoek, de pancake
panty, de tights
paraplu, de umbrella
pardon! excuse me!
pardon? pardon?
parkeerplaats, de car park; parking space
parkeren to park
Pasen Easter
paskamer, de changing room *(shop)*
paspoort, het passport
passagier, de passenger
patat, de chips
pension, het boarding house; guesthouse
per by; per

perron, het platform *(train)*
pijn, de pain; ache
pijnlijk painful
pijnstiller, de painkiller
pijp, de pipe *(smoker's)*
pikant spicy
pil, de pill; tablet
pils pilsner; lager
pincet, het tweezers
pinda, de peanut
plak, de slice *(of ham)*
plat flat; level
plattegrond, de map; plan
platteland, het countryside
plein, het square *(town)*
pleister, de sticking plaster
politie, de police
politiebureau, het police station
pond, het Britse pound *(sterling)*
pond, het Dutch pound *(weight)*; 0.5 kilo
poppenkast, de puppet show
portefeuille, de wallet
portemonnaie, de purse
postbus PO Box
postkantoor, het post office
postzegel, de stamp *(postage)*
praten to talk
precies exact
prijs, de price; prize
prijslijst, de price list
privé private
proberen to try *(attempt)*
proeven to taste
proost! cheers!

R

raam, het window
raar strange; silly
rauw raw
recentelijk recently
recept, het prescription; recipe
receptie, de reception *(desk)*
recht straight
rechtdoor straight on
rechts right *(side)*
rechtsaf gaan turn right
reddingsvest, het life jacket
regelen to arrange
regen, de rain
regenkleding, de rainclothes; waterproofs

reis, de journey; trip
reisbureau, het travel agent
reisgids, de guidebook
reizen to travel
rekening, de bill; invoice; account
relatie, de relation; relationship
rem, de brake
repareren to repair
reserve spare
reserveren to book; to reserve
reservering, de booking
restaurant, het restaurant
retour, het return ticket
reumatiek, de arthritis
rij, de line; row; queue
rijbewijs, het driving licence
rijden to drive; to ride
rijp ripe
rijst, de rice
roeien to row *(boat)*
roepen to call *(shout)*
roken to smoke
rolstoel, de wheelchair
roltrap, de escalator
rond round *(shape)*
rondkijken to browse
rondleiding, de guided tour *(in museum, etc)*
röntgenstralen, de X-rays
rood red
rook, de smoke
room, de cream *(dairy)*
roos, de rose
rot rotten *(fruit etc)*
roze pink
rug, de back *(of body)*
rugzak, de backpack; rucksack
ruiken to smell
rundvlees, het beef
rust, de rest *(repose)*
rusten to rest
rustig quiet

S

samen together
sap, het juice
saus, de sauce
schaar, de scissors
schaatsen to skate
schade, de damage
scheermes, het razor
schieten to shoot
schilderij, het painting
schoonmaken to clean

Dutch – English

schotel, de	saucer
...-schotel	served as a meal
Schotland	Scotland
Schots	Scottish
schrijven	to write
schuld	fault, guilt
serie, de	series
serieus	serious *(person)*
serveerster, de	waitress
servet, het	napkin
sinaasappelsap, het	orange juice
sla, de	lettuce
slaapkamer, de	bedroom
slaapzak, de	sleeping bag
slager, de	butcher
slapen	to sleep
slecht	bad *(weather, news)*
slechts	only
slepen	to tow
sleutel, de	key
slijter, de	off-licence
slot, het	lock; castle
sluiten	to shut
SMS	text message
smaak, de	flavour; taste
smaken	to taste *(good or bad)*
smaakt het?	is everything all right with your meal?
snackbar, de	snack bar; chip shop
sneeuw, de	snow
snelheid, de	speed
sneltrein, de	fast train
snijbonen, de	runner beans
snijden	to cut
snoep, het	sweets
soep, de	soup
soms	sometimes
soort, het	kind *(sort, type)*
speciaal	special
specialiteit, de	speciality
spiegel, de	mirror
spier, de	muscle
spoor, het	platform *(train)*
spoorweg, de	railway
spreken	to speak
stad, de	city; town
stadhuis, het	town hall
staking, de	strike
station, het	station
stekker, de	plug *(electrical)*
sterk	strong
stier, de	bull
stijl	style; steep
stil	silent; quiet; motionless
stilte, de	silence

stoel, de chair
stoep, de pavement
stoffig dusty
stomerij, de dry-cleaner's
stoofpot, de stew
stoptrein, de slow train
straat, de street
strand, het beach
streng verboden... strictly forbidden...
strijken to iron
strippenkaart, de public transport ticket *(for several trips)*
sturen to send
suiker, de sugar
suikerziekte, de diabetes
s.v.p. please *(abbreviation)*

T

taal, de language
taart, de cake
tabak, de tobacco
tafel, de table
tand, de tooth
tandarts, de dentist
tanden, de teeth
tandenstoker, de toothpick
tandpasta, de toothpaste
tarief, de price; tariff
tas, de bag
taxichauffeur, de taxi driver
taxistandplaats, de taxi rank
te at; to; in; too
te huur to let
te koop for sale
teen, de toe
tegen against
tegenover opposite
telefoon, de telephone
telefooncel, de telephone box
telefoongesprek, het telephone call/ conversation
televisie, de television
temperatuur, de temperature
tenminste at least
tentoonstelling, de exhibition
terras, het terrace
terug back
terugbetalen to refund
teruggaan to go back
teruggeven to give back
terugkomen to come back
terwijl while

teveel too much; too many
tevreden pleased
thee, de tea
theezakje, het teabag
thuis at home
tijd, de time
tijdelijk temporary
tijdens during
toegang entrance; admission
toelaten to let *(allow)*
toen then
toerist, de tourist
toeristenkaart, de tourist ticket
toeristenbelasting, de tourist tax
toeslag, de supplement
toestaan to allow
toetsenbord, het keyboard
toilet, het toilet
toiletpapier, het toilet paper
tomaat, de tomato
toren, de tower
tosti, de toasted sandwich
tot until
totaal, het total
tram, de tram
transformator, de adaptor *(electrical)*
trap, de stairs
trein, de train
trekken to pull; pull *(sign on door)*
trouwen to marry
tuin, de garden
tussen between
tv, de TV
tweede second
tweede klas second class
tweepersoonsbed, het double bed
tweepersoonskamer, de double room

U

u you *(formal, sing. and plural)*
ui, de onion
uit out; exit; off *(machine, etc)*
uitdoen to switch off
uitgang, de exit
uitnodigen to invite
uitpakken to unpack
uitslag, de rash *(on skin)*
uitspreken to pronounce

uitstappen to get off *(bus, metro, etc)*
uitverkocht sold out
uitverkoop, de sale
uitzicht, het view *(panorama)*
universiteit, de university
uur, het hour

V

vaak frequent; often
vader, de father
vakantie, de holiday
vallen to fall
van of; from
vanavond tonight
vandaag today
vanmiddag this afternoon
vanmorgen this morning
vannacht tonight
vanochtend this morning
varkensvlees, het pork
vast secure; stuck
veel much; many; a lot of
vegetariër, de vegetarian *(person)*
vegetarisch vegetarian
veilig safe
veiligheid, de safety
ventilator, de fan *(electric)*; ventilator
ver far
verandering, de change
verband, het bandage
verboden prohibited
verboden doorgang no thoroughfare
verboden toegang no entry
verdieping, de storey
verdoving, de anaesthetic
verdrietig sad
verdrinken to drown
Verenigde Staten, de United States
vergeten to forget
vergoeden to reimburse
vergunning, de licence; permit
verhuren to hire out
verjaardag, de birthday
verkeer, het traffic
verkeerd wrong
verkopen to sell
verliezen to lose
verloofd engaged *(to be married)*
verloofde, de fiancé(e)
verloren lost *(object)*
vermist missing *(person)*

verontschuldigen to excuse
verplicht compulsory
verrassing, de surprise
verschillend different
verschrikkelijk awful
vers fresh *(food)*
versnellingen, de gears
verstaan to understand *(hear)*
verstopt constipated; blocked
vertalen to translate
vertellen to tell
vertr. departure *(abbreviation)*
vertragen to delay
vertraging, de delay
vertrek, het departure
vertrekken to depart
vervelend boring

verwachten to expect
in verwachting zijn to be pregnant
verwarming, de heating
verzekering, de insurance
verzoeken to request
passagiers worden verzocht... passengers are requested to...
vet fat; greasy
via by *(via)*
vinger, de finger
vis, de fish
vissen to fish
visum, het visa
vlaai, de lattice fruit tart
Vlaams Flemish
Vlaanderen Flanders
vlakbij close by; near

vlees, het meat
vlek, de stain
vlieg, de fly
vliegveld, het airport
vloed, de flood; high tide
vlucht, de flight
vluchtstrook, de hard shoulder *(road)*
vlug quick
vochtig damp
voedselvergiftiging, de food poisoning
voelen to feel
voet, de foot
voetbal football
voetganger, de pedestrian
vogel, de bird
vol full
vol pension full board
volgen follow
volgende next

volwassene, de	adult
voor	before; in front of; for
voorbehoedsmiddel, het	contraceptive
voorbereiden	to prepare
voorgerecht, het	starter *(meal)*
voorjaar, het	spring *(season)*
voornaam, de	first name
voorrang, de	priority; right of way
geef voorrang	give way
rechts heeft voorrang	give way to traffic from right
voorruit, de	windscreen *(car)*
vooruit	in advance
voorzichtig	careful
vorig	last
vraag, de	question
vragen	to ask *(for something)*
vreemd	strange
vriend, de	(boy)friend
vriendin, de	(girl)friend
vrij	free; vacant
vrijgezel, de	bachelor
vroeg	early
vroeger	earlier
vrouw, de	woman
vruchten, de	fruits
VS	USA
vuil	dirty
vuilnis, het	litter; rubbish
vullen	to fill
vuur, het	fire
VVV	tourist information office

W

waar	true; where
waarom	why
waarschuwing, de	warning
wachten op	to wait for
wadden, de	mudflats
Waddeneilanden, de	West Frisian islands
wandelen	to walk
wandeling, de	walk
wanneer	when; if
warenhuis, het	department store
warm	warm
wassen	to wash
wat?	what?
water, het	water
watten, de	cotton wool
wc, de	toilet
we	we

Dutch – English

week, de week
weer again
weer, het weather
weg, de road; path; route
wegenkaart, de road map
wegomlegging, de diversion *(traffic)*
weinig little *(few)*
welk which
welkom welcome
welterusten! good night!; sleep well!
werkdag, de weekday
werken to work
werkloos unemployed
werkzaamheden (road) works
west west
weten to know *(facts)*
wie who
wiel, het wheel
wij we
wijn, de wine
willen to want
windmolen, de windmill
winkel, de shop
winkelen to shop
winter, de winter
wisselen to (ex)change
wisselkantoor, het bureau de change
wond, de wound; injury
wonen to live *(place)*
woordenboek, het dictionary
worst, de sausage

Y

yoghurt, de yoghurt

Z

zacht soft
zakdoek, de handkerchief
zaken, de business
zalf, de ointment
zand, het sand
ze she; they
zee, de sea
zeep, de soap
zeer sore *(pain)*; very
zeeziek seasick
zeggen to say
zeilen sailing *(sport)*
zeker certain; sure
zelfbediening self-service
zetten to put
zich oneself
ziek sick; ill
ziekenhuis, het hospital
zien see
zij she; they
zitplaats, de seat *(in bus, train)*

zitten to sit
zo so
zoals like
zoeken to look for
zoen, de kiss
zoenen to kiss
zoet sweet
zoetstof, de sweetener
zomer, de summer
zon, de sun
zonder without
zonnebaden to sunbathe
zonnebril, de sunglasses
zonnesteek, de sunstroke
zoon, de son
zorgen voor to look after
zout, het salt
zoute drop salt liquorice
zoveel so much; so many

zuid south
zuur, het pickle
zwaar heavy
zwanger pregnant
zwart black
zwembad, het swimming pool
zwemmen to swim

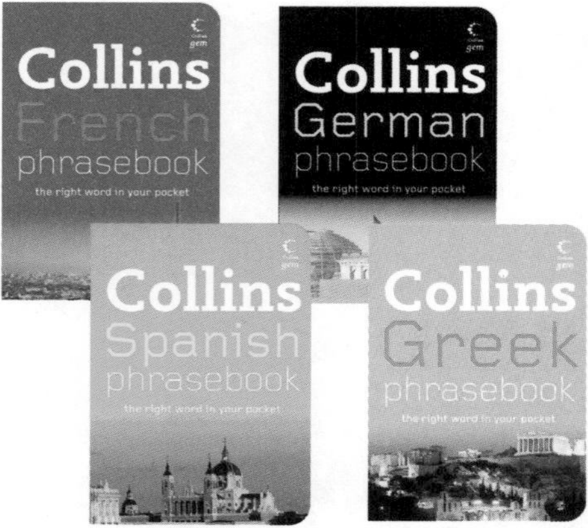

Collins Phrasebook & Dictionary

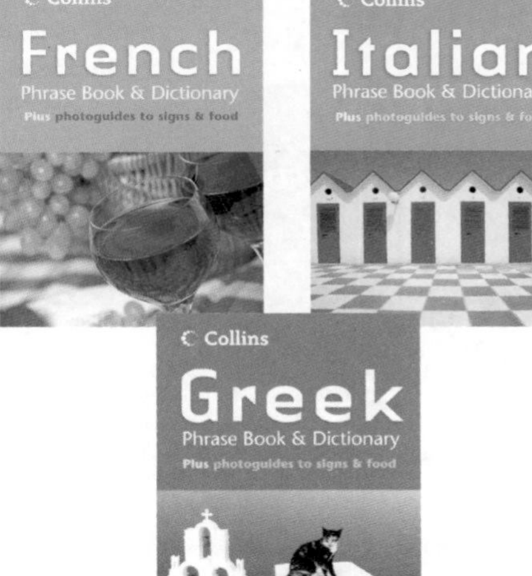

Also available as **Phrasebook CD Pack**

Other titles in the series

German Japanese Portuguese Spanish